Emotional Intelligence at Work

Emotional Intelligence at Work

A Professional Guide

(Third Edition)

Dalip Singh

Response Books
A division of Sage Publications
New Delhi/Thousand Oaks/London

Copyright © Dalip Singh, 2006, 2003, 2001

All rights reserved. No part of this book may be reproduced or utilised in any form or by any means, electronic or mechanical, including photocopying, recording, or by any information storage or retrieval system, without permission in writing from the publisher.

First published in 2001
Second revised edition published in 2003
Third revised edition published in 2006 by

Response Books
A division of Sage Publications India Pvt Ltd
B1/I-1 Mohan Cooperative Industrial Area
Mathura Road
New Delhi 110 044

Sage Publications Inc
2455 Teller Road
Thousand Oaks, California 91320

Sage Publications Ltd
1 Oliver's Yard, 55 City Road
London EC1Y 1SP

Published by Tejeshwar Singh for Response Books, Laser typeset in 11/13 points ACaslon Regular by Excellent Laser Typesetters, Delhi, and printed at Chaman Enterprises, New Delhi.

Fourth Printing 2008

Library of Congress Cataloging-in-Publication Data

Singh, Dalip, 1956–
  Emotional intelligence at work: a professional guide/Dalip Singh. — 3rd ed.
      p. cm.
  Includes bibliographical references and index.

  1. Psychology, Industrial. 2. Emotional intelligence. I. Title.

HF5548.8.S526   158.7—dc22   2006   2006030036

ISBN: 10: 0–7619–3532–0 (PB)   10: 81–7829–688–8 (India-PB)
         13: 978–0–7619–3532–2 (PB)   13: 978–81–7829–688–3 (India-PB)

Production Team: Roopa Sharma, Mathew P.J. and Santosh Rawat *for*

Jogi

Contents

List of Tables and Figures	9
Preface to the Third Revised Edition	11
Preface to the Second Revised Edition	13
Preface to the First Edition	15

1. **Emotional Intelligence: The Concept** — 19
   Introduction □ EQ makes a Difference in Life □ What Exactly is EQ? □ Are You Emotionally Intelligent? □ How Do You Acquire Your EQ? □ EQ Helps in Professional Success □ Some Myths about EQ

2. **Emotional Intelligence and Your Personality** — 51
   The Relationship between EQ and IQ □ Where Do Emotions Come From? □ Consequences of Low and High EQ

3. **Can EQ be Developed?** — 59
   Early Life Experiences □ EQ Develops with Maturity □ A Case Study □ Emotions can be Unlearned □ Examples of EQ Development

4. **Emotional Skills that Managers should Learn** — 73
   Learn to Recognise Your Emotions □ Learn to Empathise with Others □ Develop High Self-esteem □ Manage Emotional Upsets □ Be an Emotional 'Winner' □ Learn the Art of Influencing People □ Manage Your Anger □ Other Related Areas

5. **Emotional Intelligence: The Empirical Evidence** — 103
   Defining Emotional Intelligence □ Levels of EQ Required for Various Jobs □ Emotional Intelligence Competencies

◻ EQ in the Indian Perspective ◻ Do Different Professions Require Different Levels of EQ? ◻ Emotional Intelligence of IAS Officers ◻ Emotional Intelligence and Leadership Behaviour ◻ Relation between EQ and IQ among Adolescents ◻ EQ and Managerial Effectiveness: An International Study ◻ EQ and Well-being of Adolescents ◻ The Soft Art of being a Tough Leader ◻ Emotional Intelligence and Stress Management ◻ Managing Human Capital: An EQ Perspective ◻ The Making of an EQ Test ◻ Other Research Studies

6. **Guidelines for Training and Development** — 192
Phase One: Preparation for Change ◻ Phase Two: Training ◻ Phase Three: Transfer and Maintenance ◻ Phase Four: Evaluating Change

7. **Know Your EQ: Emotional Quotient Test** — 210
The EQ Test (Developed by N.K. Chadha and Dalip Singh)

References and Select Bibliography — 223
Index — 226
About the Author — 236

List of Tables and Figures

Tables

1.1	Traditionalists versus Modernists	28
2.1	Consequences of Levels of EQ	57
5.1	Level of EQ Required for Various Jobs	114
5.2	Framework of Emotional Competencies	116
5.3	Study on Postgraduate and Undergraduate Students	126
5.4	Frequency of Response	127
5.5	The Results	135
5.6	Clusters and Professions	136
5.7	Mean and Standard Deviation (N = 60) on the Variable of Emotional Intelligence	143
5.8	Comparison between Group I and Group II IAS Officers	143
5.9	EQ Level of IAS Officers	143
5.10	Means, SDs and Intercorrelations (N = 150)	167
5.11	Means, SDs and F-ratios	173
5.12	Summary of Stepwise Discriminator Analysis	175

Figures

1.1	Indicator of a Person's Success in Life	26
1.2	The Personality	33
1.3	The Individual	39
1.4	EQ Gets You Promoted!	44

2.1	The Human Mind	54
5.1	Dimensions of Emotional Intelligence	127
5.2	Defining Emotional Intelligence	128
5.3	Professions	137
5.4	EQ Level	144
5.5	Comparison of Four Groups on the Variable 'Emotional Intelligence'	160
5.6	Comparison of Four Groups on the Variable 'Managerial Effectiveness'	162

Preface to the Third Revised Edition

It is a matter of immense satisfaction for me that the first and second editions of the book were bestsellers. This has motivated me to bring the third revised and thoroughly refreshed edition before the readers. The concept of emotional intelligence or emotional quotient (EQ) has also gained popularity and acceptance over the years. How well do you connect with yourself and with others? Your ability to appropriately identify, recognise and manage your emotions for your own well-being as well as the well-being of people around you is what is described as emotional intelligence. Your emotional sensitivity, maturity and competency is what ultimately decides your destiny. Can you recognise your emotions and control them to your advantage, can you make out how your behaviour is affecting the people around you? Do you know how to handle stress, frustration, anxiety and conflict? Can you make out the most out of the situations whether good or bad?

The third edition tends to answer some of the questions: What is emotional intelligence? What does it look like? What are it's different components, and how are they related? How is it different from other concepts? In what ways and to what extent do improvements in emotional intelligence enhance individual, group and organisational performance? You will find answers to all the above in this revised and re-researched book.

An important objective of this edition is to promote high-quality research on the application of emotional intelligence in organisations. In order to advance this objective, practical applications of EQ in organisations have been given in this edition.

This book has all the answers to the situations you may have be pondering over in the recent past. This book will help you to know what emotional intelligence is, specific areas in which EQ may be applied, specific recommendations about how to develop your EQ and what skills you should master to be emotionally intelligent. The practical aspect of the third edition is that you will discover what your current level of EQ is and what you can do to further develop it. I hope the book contributes in upgrading the EQ of individuals, organisations and the society as a whole and lead to the betterment of mankind.

The Website on the book www.eqindia.com has also been very popular. It attracted hundreds of visitors from all over the globe, who attempted online EQ test. The data so compiled has further been used to define emotional intelligence.

I would like to place on record my gratitude to Professor N.K. Chadha, University of Delhi, for his heartfelt involvement in my research work.

Chandigarh, India   **DALIP SINGH**
2006

Preface to the Second Revised Edition

The workplace is not the right place for emotions—that was the conventional wisdom. Emotions were disruptive and had to be reined in, buttoned up and locked away. If they were turned loose, it would wreck the discipline in organisations and the carefully crafted order that had been nurtured over the years.

However, the growing body of research in the US on emotional intelligence and emotional quotient (EQ) in the mid-eighties has turned the tide, making organisations and the people who work there less wary of dealing with emotions.

Funnily enough, Indians who deal with a variety of emotions in their daily lives seem to zipper up their emotive side as soon as they enter their workplaces. This is prompted by the mistaken notion that work is serious business and any display of emotion ought to be regarded with extreme suspicion.

This revised edition is indicative of two things: first, that attitudes in Indian organisations are beginning to change and managers are no longer sidling down corporate corridors afraid to tread on someone's 'emotive' corns; second, there have been a lot of fast-paced developments in this field since the first edition of this book came out just over a year ago.

There has been tremendous interest in the subject in universities, the business world, and among the general public. The book itself has done good business in India, Europe and America, which is pretty gratifying. A number of doctoral studies have also been carried out in the field signifying its value in the academic world.

This revised edition gives the book a distinctive Indian orientation. To start with I have evolved an Indian definition of emotional intelligence based on the extensive research I have carried out in industry and elsewhere. My model of emotional intelligence consists of three major dimensions emotional competence, emotional maturity and emotional sensitivity. Based on these dimensions, I have defined emotional intelligence as 'the ability of an individual to appropriately and successfully respond to a variety of emotional stimuli elicited from the inner self and the immediate environment. Emotional intelligence constitutes these three psychological dimensions which motivate an individual to recognise truthfully, interpret honestly and handle tactfully the dynamics of human behaviour.'

The definition captures the Indian psyche and I am sure that it will be of immense use to Indian researchers, corporates and the general public.

In the revised edition, I have incorporated two new chapters—one containing the latest Indian research in the field and the other drawing lessons for the modern-day manager from the Bhagvad Gita. While we are looking at the exciting developments in the field, I have tried to ensure that we do not lose sight of the body of wisdom in our ancient sacred texts. This will help a manager deal with emotional conflict, troubleshooting, stress and burnout situations in everyday life.

I am sure that the fresh contents will be appreciated by the readers and will also lead to quality research in this field.

Chandigarh, India **DALIP SINGH**
2003

Preface to the First Edition

What determines professional success? Is it primarily your intelligence level or intelligence quotient (IQ), or is it your personality characteristics, or is it a combination of several things? I have pondered over this question for several years without arriving at a convincing answer. According to the proponents of emotional intelligence (EQ), a person's emotional make-up largely determines his or her professional success. They believe that EQ is the most important determinant of the extent of professional and personal success in life. It is interesting to note that so many people with high IQ fail whereas those with less intellectual endowment are extremely successful. Even in certain renowned business establishments, where people are trained to be smart, the most valued and productive managers are those who have a high emotional intelligence level, and not necessarily those with the highest IQ. Such examples abound in business, politics, academia and administration. It is increasingly recognised that IQ may account for only about 20 per cent of a person's success in life. The remaining 80 per cent depends largely on a person's emotional intelligence, i.e., EQ.

The leitmotif of this book is that the rules for work are constantly changing. People are being judged by a new yardstick: how well they are able to handle themselves and others and not merely in terms of their academic qualifications and expertise. This yardstick is increasingly being applied to decisions regarding the hiring and firing of employees, who will be retained and who will be sidelined and who will be promoted. It is said that in the corporate world a person is recruited on the basis of his or her IQ, but is promoted on the grounds of his or her EQ. These new rules predict who is most likely to become a successful manager and who is most prone to failure. Whatever a person's vocation, he or she is being measured for traits which are crucial to his or her future marketability.

These rules have little to do with what you were taught as important in school and college. The new measures take it for granted that you have the requisite IQ and technical know-how to do your job: it focuses instead on personal qualities, such as initiative and empathy, motivation and awareness, all of which constitute EQ.

Simply put, EQ denotes 'Emotional Quotient' and is used interchangeably with 'Emotional Intelligence', a term derived from 'Intelligence Quotient' (IQ). In a layperson's language this could be defined as knowing what feels good, what feels bad, and how to get from bad to good. A more formal academic definition refers to emotional awareness and emotional management skills, which enable you to balance emotion and reason so as to maximise your long-term happiness. Emotional intelligence includes qualities such as self-awareness, ability to manage moods, motivation, empathy and social skills like cooperation and leadership.

Your level of emotional intelligence is neither genetically fixed, nor does it develop only in early childhood. Unlike IQ, which does not increase after adolescence, emotional intelligence is largely learned and continues to develop throughout life and is conditioned by life's experiences. Unlike IQ, emotional intelligence can be improved throughout life. In the normal course of a lifetime, emotional intelligence tends to increase as you learn to be more aware of your moods, to effectively handle distressing emotions, and to listen and empathise. In short, as you become more mature, you can acquire certain emotional competencies that lead to outstanding performance at work.

Some of the negative emotions which require emotional management and regulation are anger, failure, fear, disappointment, frustration, obligation, guilt, resentment, emptiness, bitterness, dependence, depression, loneliness and lethargy. Similarly, positive emotions such as motivation, appreciation, friendship, self-control, satisfaction, freedom, fulfilment, autonomy, peace, desire, awareness, contentment, elation and happiness can be used effectively as and when the situation demands.

Why is it necessary to develop EQ? The reason is that people with high EQ are happier, healthier and more successful in their relationships. These people strike a balance between emotion and reason, are aware of their own feelings, show empathy and compassion for others, and have high self-esteem. Emotional intelligence can be instrumental in many situations in the workplace and can help achieve organisational effectiveness. On the basis of advanced research on the requirements of a CEO's office, psychologists concluded that in the fast-changing corporate environment you need more than just brains to run your business. You also need high EQ for making the right decisions and solving problems. Some of the immediate benefits of high EQ are that it can lead to increased productivity, enhanced leadership skills, improved responsiveness and greater creativity. It can also create an enthusiastic work environment, reduce stress levels and resolve emotional issues, improve the well-being of employees and improve relationships all round. EQ can enable employees to resolve past issues and both external as well as internal conflicts, help them attain emotional power and accomplish their goals at all levels physical, mental, emotional and spiritual and improve psychological abilities such as memory, clarity of thinking and decision-making.

Increasingly, more companies are realising that encouraging emotional intelligence skills is a vital component of their management philosophy. An organisation does not compete with products alone: how well it uses its people is more important for its survival. The Consortium for Research on Emotional Intelligence in Organisations has illustrated how emotional intelligence contributes to the bottom line in any work organisation. EQ can be a valuable tool for HR practitioners and managers who need to bring about changes in their own organisations. It is being increasingly recognised that EQ can be effectively applied to the unique requirements of any organisation. The principles of EQ can help employees become better team players, show greater creativity in their work and increase overall productivity through the powerful techniques of integrating and applying emotional intelligence at the workplace. For example, learning how to successfully overcome obstacles and blocks, resolve conflicts and deal with any issue that may come in the way of accomplishing managerial objectives.

What are the ramifications of EQ for a professional? Clearly, in any discussion of emotional intelligence, it is important to identify the key determinants of success in the workplace. Even more important is the basis on which you form your personal compass, both at the workplace and elsewhere. Having been exposed to the psychological aspects of EQ, readers would want to assess their own EQ level. To help readers measure their EQ 'Emotional Intelligence Test', standardised and developed by Professor N.K. Chadha of the University of Delhi, has been included in the book. I am sure that readers will find it informative and interesting.

This work could not have been completed without the active support of a large number of friends and well-wishers. It is not possible to name them all and acknowledge their contribution individually. However, I am particularly grateful to Professor N.K. Chadha, Payal Mehta, Professor John Van Willigen of Kentucky University, Professors H.C. Ganguli, N.R. Chatterjee, V.K. Bhalla of the University of Delhi, and Ravi Bangar, S.P. Mahi and Satish Parashar, to name just a few.

It is my fervent hope that the book will lead to improved interpersonal relations at the workplace, within the family and elsewhere.

DALIP SINGH

1

Emotional Intelligence: The Concept

> Anyone can be angry—that is easy. But to be angry with the right person, to the right degree, at the right time, for the right purpose, and in the right way—that is not easy.
> —*Aristotle*

INTRODUCTION

What do love, happiness, fear, affection, hate, shame, disgust, surprise, sadness, elation and anger have in common? These are emotions that directly affect your day-to-day life. For long, it has been believed that success at the workplace depends on your level of intelligence or intelligence quotient (IQ) as reflected in your academic achievements, exams passed, marks obtained, and so on. In other words, your intellectual credentials are: doing well in school, holding an engineering degree or even an advanced computer degree, obtaining high scores in an IQ test. All these are instances of intelligence of the academic variety. But how smart are you outside the classroom, faced with life's difficult moments? Here, you need a different kind of resourcefulness. You need, what is called, emotional intelligence or emotional quotient (EQ), which is a different way of being smart.

Why is it that the smartest people are not always the wealthiest, and why are some people instantly liked upon introduction, while

---

For the sake of clarity the terms emotional intelligence (EI) and emotional quotient (EQ) will be used interchangeably throughout the book.

others are distrusted? Why are some people sympathetic and caring, and have a rich and fulfilling emotional life? Why are some people comfortable with themselves and the social universe they inhabit, while many others are not? Why do some people, with less academic achievements, lead a fulfilling life, whereas many people with high IQ, make their own life, and those of people around them, miserable?

Emotional intelligence is what gives a person the competitive edge. Even in certain renowned business establishments, where everyone is trained to be smart, the most valued and productive managers are those who have strong traits of emotional intelligence. Being endowed with great intellectual abilities, you may become a brilliant fiscal analyst or a legal scholar, but a highly developed emotional intelligence is what will make you a candidate for a CEO, a brilliant trial lawyer, a successful politician or a powerful bureaucrat. Your EQ constitutes factors that are most likely to ensure success in your marriage or your love affair, or that you attain dizzy heights in your business. The lack of emotional intelligence explains why people who, despite having a high IQ, have been failures in their personal and professional lives.

Today, the rules of the workplace are rapidly changing; a new yardstick is being used to judge people. It is often said that a high IQ may assure you a top position, but it may not make you a top person. This does not measure how smart you are or what your academic qualifications are or even what your expertise is. Instead, it measures how well you are able to handle yourself and others. This yardstick is increasingly applied in deciding who will be hired and who will not, who will be dismissed and who will be retained, who will be ignored and who will be promoted. These new rules predict who is most likely to be successful and who is most likely to fail. Regardless of the field you are currently working in, you are being judged for emotional traits that are crucial to your marketability for future jobs or new assignments. Possibly, employees of large organisations may be evaluated in terms of such abilities, even though they may not be aware of it. If you are applying for a job, you are likely to be assessed in terms of these emotional abilities, though no one will tell you so explicitly.

Whatever the job, understanding how to cultivate these abilities is essential for a successful career.

These emotional traits have little to do with what you were told was important in school, college or other institutions; academic abilities are largely irrelevant to these new standards. Today, it is taken for granted that you have adequate IQ, that is, the intellectual ability and the technical know-how to do your job. The focus, instead, is on your EQ—personal qualities such as initiative, empathy, motivation and leadership. To illustrate this point further, it may be said that people involved in the same profession generally fall above a certain threshold of intelligence or IQ. For example, few physicians are of average intelligence since they must have an IQ above a certain level to make it through medical college. Some managers are smarter than others. But none are dumb. This is where the question arises of how to differentiate between managers who have more or less similar levels of IQ. It is here that EQ becomes important for it sets apart people with similar IQs. This is neither a passing fad nor a temporary management credo. Data obtained from studies of working people confirm that emotional capabilities need to be taken seriously in order to be a star performer. At a time when there are no guarantees of job security and when the very concept of a 'job' is being rapidly replaced by 'portable skills' or 'marketable skills', EQ is considered as the prime factor which makes and keeps people employable. Although these 'intelligent' qualities have for decades been referred to by various names—from 'smartness' and 'personality' to 'soft skills' and 'competence'—it is only now that there is a precise understanding of these emotional abilities and a new name given to it: emotional intelligence or emotional quotient (EQ).

If you work for a small organisation or are self-employed, your ability to perform at your peak may depend to a large extent on your having these emotional abilities, though these were definitely not taught at school or college. Even so, your career will depend to a greater or lesser extent on how well you are able to master these abilities. If you are working for a large organisation, you have to see if your organisation fosters such competencies or discourages them. The effectiveness and productivity of the organisation will depend upon the degree of acceptance of these emotional competencies.

In the 1970s and 1980s, people got ahead by attending the 'right' schools and performing 'well' in written exams or competitions. Today, the world has thousands of well-trained, promising men and women who have reached their plateau or, worse, have failed because of crucial gaps in their emotional competencies. Today, for a new entry-level employee, specific technical skills are less important than an underlying ability to learn on the job. You need 'marketable skills' in addition to your academic achievements. The qualities which are considered crucial by employers these days are many: listening and verbal communication, adaptability and creative responses to setbacks and obstacles, personal management, confidence, motivation to work towards goals, a sense of wanting to develop one's career and taking pride in accomplishments, group and inter-personal effectiveness, co-operation and teamwork, skills in solving disagreements, willingness to make a contribution, leadership potential, along with competencies in reading, writing and mathematics. Of these desirable traits, only reading, writing and mathematics are academic skills. All the others are related to the non-academic arena—to emotional intelligence. What corporations now seek in the new entrants they hire are EQ qualities.

Let us see some illustrations to better understand this: 'I had the lowest grade point average ever in my school,' says a senior army officer. 'But when I joined the army I was graded number one by my superiors. It was all about how you handled yourself, got along with people, worked in teams, motivated others, inspired leadership, and so on. And I found this to be true at the workplace.' According to a senior civil servant, 'Too many young officers can't take criticism. They are too sensitive and have a fragile ego. They get defensive or hostile when seniors give them feedback on how they are doing. They react to performance feedback as though it were a personal attack.'

If the answer is 'no' to one or more of these questions, your problem has been diagnosed. You are a normal, average, thinking person trained by family, school and workplace to value IQ (the

> ☞ **Before you move ahead, answer a few simple questions:**
>
> - Do you assess your personal and professional life at the moment as satisfactory?
> - Have you achieved all your expected goals?
> - Are you content with the number of friends you have and the depth of your friendships?
> - Is your marriage the fountain of intimacy and support you dreamed it would be?
> - Have you been promoted with the readiness and speed you deserved at work?
> - Do you generally feel at ease with the world or a little out of place?

head) and devalue EQ (the heart). You have learned to suppress your feelings, emotions and passions, and use your head rather than your heart to find out what your body feels and wants. In short, you use your IQ, and not EQ, to solve your problems. It is not possible to feel comfortable at the workplace if you are not comfortable in your own skin. Once you have learned to accept your emotional self, every facet of your work life will benefit. You may have noticed that the price you pay for ignoring your emotions is far too high. The cost is depriving yourself of the emotional skills you need for a healthy, satisfying and fulfilling life. Your IQ may help you in understanding and dealing with the world at one level, but you need emotions to understand and deal with yourself and, in turn, with others. It is not possible to get along well with others, and get ahead in the world regardless of how 'academically smart' you are, if you are unaware of your emotions and not able to recognise and value them, and act honestly with them. In short, you are often simply at sea, out of touch with your sense of self. Feeling your emotions is certainly not a sign of weakness. You follow strict rules on how, when, where and how much you should allow yourself to express

> It is not possible to feel comfortable at the workplace if you are not comfortable in your own skin.

emotions because you have been told to do so. If you cry, you do not do so in front of others. When you are angry, you bite your tongue. When you are hurt, you force a smile. Unfortunately, however, such actions backfire. It is healthy for the mind, body, heart and spirit to experience emotions when they arise. Otherwise emotions can be self-destructive. Most strong emotions do not last long at all. If you do not suppress your emotions, you will have a clear head, a contented heart, and greater self-control. If you fight them, they will haunt you.

☞ The Marshmallow Experiment

For most of the 20th century, scientists have worshipped the hardware powers of the brain, but there has not been any significant attempt to study the software powers of the heart. Walter Mischel, a psychologist at Stanford University, took up the challenge and studied the value of emotional intelligence. He, like many of us, wanted to know the answers to certain perplexing questions: why some people seem to have a gift for living well; why the smartest kid in the class may not end up as the richest; why some people are liked almost instantly and others are distrusted; why some people remain buoyant in the face of troubles which would sink a less resilient soul. In short, what are the qualities of brain and heart that determine success. He decided to conduct a psychological experiment on small children to find out the real story.

> The ability to delay gratification is a master skill, a triumph of the brain's reasoning power over its impulsive one.

Mischel distributed marshmallows (a kind of sweet) to groups of 4-year-olds and left the room, promising that any child who could postpone eating the marshmallows until he came back, 15 to 20 minutes later, would be rewarded with a second marshmallow. Not all the children, however, behaved or followed his instructions identically. Some of them just could not resist the temptation to eat the marshmallow immediately. Some waited for a few minutes, and then decided that there was no fun in waiting for a second one, and

Contd.

Contd.

that it would be wiser to eat the one which was in hand. Some fantacised with closed eyes that they were eating the marshmallows and tried to wait for the return of Mischel. Significantly, there were still some kids who did not allow tempting thought(s) to sway them, and did not touch the marshmallows at all till Mischel returned. This experiment further reported that some of the children had been able to think differently. They had resorted to singing, tapping their feet, telling themselves stories, and imagining that the marshmallow was a fluffy cloud, to avoid eating it. Interestingly enough, one kid had even fallen asleep with the marshmallow in his hand! Mischel came to the conclusion that the different moods of the children reflected the amount of emotional intelligence they exhibited. Does this experiment really provide a fundamental measure of emotional intelligence? What does it shows us to prove the importance of emotional intelligence?

Follow-up studies by Mischel 12–14 years later revealed that the children who had triumphed over their desire to delay eating the marshmallows had grown more socially competent and self-assertive and exhibited a higher degree of resilience in dealing with life's frustrations. Those who had won the second marshmallow were still better at delayed gratification and had applied this attribute in pursuit of their goals. Those who had given in to their desire and had eaten the first marshmallow immediately without waiting, had grown into more stubborn, indecisive and stressed adolescents. The quality of self-control in avoiding eating the marshmallow at the age of 4 turned out to be twice as powerful a predictor of later success in life as compared to IQ. In this experiment, the ability to delay gratification of eating the marshmallow was seen as a master skill, a triumph of the reasoning of the brain over the emotions of the heart.

The conclusion derived from this classical experiment is that the capacity to put off rewards is a single skill that psychologists pinpoint as an indicator of success in life. Mischel's study confirmed that emotional intelligence does not show up in IQ tests and needs to be viewed from an entirely different angle. The marshmallow experiment established that emotional intelligence matters more than anything else in determining success in life.

The most widely reported background paper on EQ is the Marshmallow experiment conducted in the US in the 1960s. The findings of this classical experiment help us to better understand EQ.

EQ MAKES A DIFFERENCE IN LIFE

Emotional Quotient is synergistic with Intelligence Quotient; top performers have both. The more complex the job, the more important is emotional intelligence, if only because a deficiency in these abilities can hinder the use of whatever technical expertise or intellect a person may have. EQ has ramifications for how people operate at the workplace in relation to others. For example, a manager who is unaware of his impact on others is a walking disaster at the workplace. There is a story of how one manager so intimidated others that they never gave him honest feedback.

> A manager who is unaware of his/her impact on others is a walking disaster at the workplace.

Research shows that IQ accounts for only about 20 per cent of a person's success in life. The balance can be attributed to EQ, as shown in the Figure 1.1.

Considering how much emphasis schools, colleges and other institutions place on IQ alone, it is surprising that only a small part of a person's achievement at work, or in life, is explained by

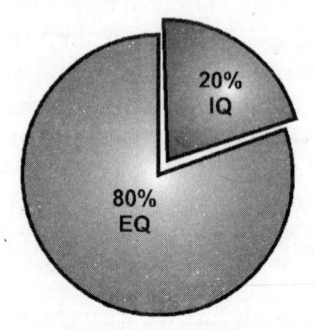

FIGURE 1.1: Indicator of a Person's Success in Life

IQ. When IQ test scores are correlated with how well people perform in life, the highest estimate of how much difference IQ makes is only about 20 per cent. This means that IQ alone leaves about 80 per cent of job success unexplained. As much as 80 per cent of success is said to be derived from EQ. In other words, IQ alone does not determine who will succeed and who will fail. For example, a study of Harvard graduates in the fields of law, medicine, teaching and business observed that scores on entrance exams, a surrogate for IQ, had zero or negative correlation with their eventual career success. Paradoxically, IQ was found to have limited power in predicting the success of people smart enough to handle the most demanding fields, and the value of emotional intelligence was found to be higher for entry into particular fields. In MBA programmes, engineering, law, or medicine, where professional selection focused almost exclusively on IQ, EQ carried far more weight than IQ in determining who emerged successful.

The difference between those at the high and low ends of emotional intelligence is very large indeed. Being at the top therefore confers a major competitive advantage. Hence, 'soft' skills matter even more for success in 'hard' fields. It has been argued that traditional academic aptitude, school grades and advanced credentials simply did not predict how well people would perform on the job or whether they would succeed in life. Instead, there is a set of specified competencies like empathy and initiative which distinguished the most successful from those who were merely good enough to retain their jobs. All these data indicate a common core of personal and social abilities as the key ingredient of emotional intelligence.

You may have noticed by now that EQ has two diverse viewpoints. There are 'traditionalists' who feel that emotions play a negative role and 'modernists' who advocate that emotions play a positive role. The impact of EQ may be evaluated by differentiating traditional performers from high performers, as shown in Table 1.1.

To elaborate this point further, let us look into the tale of two IAS officers.

TABLE 1.1: Traditionalists versus Modernists

Traditionalists believe that emotions	Modernists believe that emotions
Distract us	Motivate us
Make us vulnerable	Make us confident
Cloud our judgment	Speed our analysis
Must be controlled	Build trust
Inhibit information	Provide feedback

☞ A Tale of Two IAS Officers

Ravi and Sunil joined the premier Indian Administrative Service (IAS) about the same time, with almost the same credentials. Both had superb grade point averages from leading schools and universities, with effusive recommendations from their professors. Both went for identical professional training at the IAS Training Academy as probationers. However, the moment they joined their respective postings as fresh magistrates, all similarities disappeared.

Ravi's curriculum vitae was impressive; he was academically brilliant and a top scorer. He was a talented and creative student in his school and college days. But he acted as though he had not left high school. The problem with Ravi was that he knew he was exceptional, and was unbelievably arrogant. Despite his academic abilities, he put people off, especially those who had to work with him. He remained glued to his computer screen, voraciously devouring administrative and technical documents and learning about the rules and regulations of bureaucracy. His colleagues rarely saw him except at formal meetings; he was a recluse. He believed that it was his administrative and technical proficiency that counted most in this job. Ravi's arrogance came across all too quickly; he ended up being transferred every six months, and that too in second or third-tier outfits. And he always wondered why such things should happen to him.

Sunil, on the other hand, adopted a different approach. Though brilliant academically, he ranked slightly below Ravi in the written exams, but he was adept interpersonally. Everyone who worked with him liked him. A few years later, Sunil was termed a 'successful'

Contd.

Contd.

officer. He not only devoted adequate time to his work, but also used his spare time to get to know his co-officers, find out about their interests, projects and concerns. When they needed a helping hand, he offered one. Whenever an additional responsibility was given to him, he volunteered to do so with grace and enthusiasm. He believed that one of the most effective ways for him to be accepted into the team was by helping out.

After a few years on the job, Ravi had done slightly better as an administrator. But Sunil was seen as someone who could work well in a team and take initiatives, and was already marked out for the fast track. Ravi failed to realise that building bonds was a crucial competence for his job. His co-officers knew that he was administratively adept, but they had little faith in his ability to work in a team. In contrast, Sunil showed excellence in several emotional intelligence competencies. If Ravi's academic skills were to be put to best use, he needed to master emotional competencies as well.

There is a crucial difference between declarative knowledge, that is, knowing a concept and its technical details, and practical knowledge, that is, being able to implement these concepts. Knowing does not equal doing, whether in playing a game, managing a team, or acting on essential advice at the right moment or doing an IAS job. Ravi lacked what Sunil had—emotional intelligence. Needless to say, a modern approach based on EQ is more likely to result in higher levels of performance than a traditional approach based on IQ. It is for you to decide which path you wish to follow.

What Exactly is EQ?

The phrase 'Emotional Quotient' is being used extensively these days: for instance, in magazines which challenge you to 'know your EQ', on Internet sites which offer to test your emotional intelligence, in organisations where CEOs have started taking lessons in EQ and in offices where employees want to learn how to understand their bosses. Parents want to know why their children do not understand them, spouses discuss ways and means to tackle marital disputes, youths wonder why their circle of friend is shrinking by the day and many others discovering that they are immensely unpopular in their peer circle. Managers study how to work with subordinates, parents take courses on rearing children, husbands and wives learn to talk to each other, teachers study how to cope with emotional disturbances among their students, young minds learn to improve their interpersonal relations with peer groups. Everyone wishes to enhance emotional competencies and is asking how to do it.

Before defining 'emotional intelligence', it would be desirable to define the term 'emotion'. Interestingly, we all intuitively understand what the word 'emotion' means, but there is no generally accepted theory of emotions among psychologists though there are areas of agreement. Feelings are what one experiences as the result of having emotions. Psychologists have described and explained 'emotion' differently, but all agree that it is a complex state of the human mind involving a wide range of bodily changes such as breathing, pounding heart, flushed face, sweaty palms, high pulse rate and glandular secretions. Mentally, it is a state of excitement or perturbation marked by strong feelings.

> Emotions are human beings' warning systems that alert them to what is really going on around them. They are a complex state of the human mind, involving physiological changes on the one hand and psychological changes on the other.

Emotions originate from exposure to specific situations. Emotions, when combined with the thinking process, result in the experience of feelings; they are human beings' warning systems that alert them to what is really going on around them. Emotions are also like an internal gyroscope that helps keep us on the right track by ensuring that we are guided more by EQ and less by IQ. What is most important for each one of us is to learn to create our own emotions. Our responses are governed by our thoughts, by what we tell ourselves. As we clarify our understanding of our own beliefs and patterns, we learn that we are actually choosing our own lives. We take responsibility for our thoughts, emotions and actions; we become accountable. Emotion is an 'umbrella term' which includes the situation, the interpretation and the perception of a situation, and the response or feeling related to that situation.

In the most literal dictionary sense, emotion is defined as 'any agitation or disturbance of mind, passion; any vehement or excited mental state'. Emotion refers to a response with its distinctive thoughts, psychological and biological states and ranges of propensities to act. Generally, there are two dimensions of emotions:

Physiological Dimension	Psychological Dimension
Emotion is a complex state of human mind, involving bodily changes of widespread nature such as breathing, pounding heart, flushed face, sweating palms, pulse rate, glandular secretions, etc.	Emotion is a state of excitement or perturbation marked by strong feelings. The 'feelings', are what one experiences as the result of having emotions.

There are hundreds of emotions, along with their blends, variations, mutations and nuances. Cross-cultural studies have identified various quite distinct and universally felt emotions. Indeed, there are more subtleties in emotions than there are words to express them. For example, some of the main emotions, with their blends, have been categorised as follows:

Anger: Fury, outrage, charged, resentment, wrath, exasperation, indignation, vexation, acrimony, animosity, annoyance, irritability, hostility and, at the extreme, pathological hatred and violence.

Depression: Grief, aloofness, sorrow, cheerlessness, gloom, melancholy, self-pity, loneliness, dejection, despair and sadness.

Anxiety: Fear, apprehension, nervousness, upset, misgiving, wariness, qualm, dread, fright, terror, as a psychopathology, phobia and panic.

Happiness: Enjoyment, cheerfulness, joy, relief, contentment, bliss, delight, amusement, pride, sensual pleasure, thrill, rapture, gratification, satisfaction, euphoria, ecstasy and, at the extreme, mania.

Love: Acceptance, mutual attraction, friendliness, trust, kindness, affinity, devotion, adoration and infatuation.

Surprise: Shock, astonishment, amazement and wonder.
Disgust: Contempt, pity, disdain, scorn, abhorrence, aversion, distaste and revulsion.
Embarrassment: Shame, guilt, chagrin, remorse, humiliation, regret and mortification.

To be sure, the above list does not resolve all the questions regarding how emotions can be categorised. For example, what about blends that include jealousy, a variant of anger, with sadness and fear? Or, what of virtues such as hope and faith, courage and forgiveness, certainty and equanimity? Or, what of some of the more classic vices such as doubt, complacence and boredom? There are no clear answers, and the psychological debate on how to classify emotions continues.

> Emotions are our responses to the world around us, and they are created by the combination of our thoughts, feelings and actions. There are hundreds of emotions, along with their blends, variations, mutations and nuances.

Having known what emotions mean, let us try and understand how we use emotions in daily life by taking a look at these simple statements:

- *My boss is always in a hostile mood.*
- *The production manager is always nagging others.*
- *The manager does not understand the feelings of others.*
- *The officer blurts things out without thinking of others.*
- *She is jealous of her colleagues.*
- *Don't trust him. He is too manipulative.*
- *Management is way out of touch with employees' emotions.*
- *The new manager is too sensitive; he takes everything too personally.*

These statements refer to various blends of emotions as reflected through personality characteristics. These are fundamental to moods, nature, lifestyle and to the whole personality. The above statements indicate that EQ is the ability to understand other people: what motivates them, how they work, what are their goals.

In other words, we now know that successful politicians, bureaucrats, professionals and leaders are all likely to exhibit high levels of EQ. On the other hand, persons with low EQ are judged to be misfits in a social set-up.

To understand your EQ better, imagine that there are two parts to your personality: (*a*) a thinking part, and (*b*) a feeling part, as depicted in Figure 1.2.

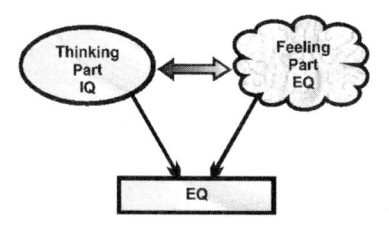

FIGURE 1.2: The Personality

These two parts communicate with each other and react in case of disagreement. It is the harmonious compatibility of the two components that constitutes EQ.

Are You Emotionally Intelligent?

Many people are extraordinarily talented, conceptually brilliant and have a very high IQ. They excel in computers, science and mathematics. Sadly though, they are not particularly likeable people. Many of them are aggressive and brutal in their responses to the outside world. They have little or no feelings for people around them. They feel psychologically awkward in relationships, have no social graces or even a social or personal life. Being uncomfortable with themselves and making people around them uncomfortable becomes a routine response in their life. Usually they are not close with any one, nor do they have any meaningful friendships. They work all the time, their one-dimension lives centred around themselves, little knowing that life cannot be lived without relating with others. Such negative traits are fatal handicaps even for high-IQ managers with sound technical knowledge.

☞ The One-dimensional Vice Chancellor

I remember an instance where the Governor-cum-Chancellor of a University had gone on annual inspection of a University. The University, which was earlier known as the 'Oxford of India', was in shambles, to say the least. There were problems relating to poor teaching standards, inefficient non-teaching staff and aggressive students' unions. During his inspection, the Chancellor decided to meet everyone individually and hear them out. Various pressure groups had different grievances ranging from recruitment, selection and promotion to immediate improvement in the University's academic and campus culture.

It turned out that the Vice Chancellor (VC) was a technocrat, a scientist of repute. He had been in the chair for over a year and had another two years of stay. One professor described the VC thus: 'He is a great strategic thinker with an ability to achieve in life but he lashes out at people around him. He is smart but his superiority demeans others. Many of us have tried to help him improve on this weakness but there seems to be no behavioral change as he refuses to accept the psychological realities.' The Chancellor soon understood the problem. The VC was an introvert, inept at handling the varied and mammoth responsibilities as also the diverse socio-political-personnel culture of the University. The VC believed that the world started and ended with him. He did not believe in allowing anyone to express any views in the University. He was not open to suggestions or criticism, not even positive ones. A month after taking this assignment, he passed an 'astonishing' order: no one could meet him during office hours as employees were expected to work at that time. And after office hours, he himself was not available to mitigate the grievances!

The students', teachers' and other unions had a simple request to make to the Chancellor. 'Please advise the VC to meet us and look into our grievances empathetically. Even if he is not in a position to solve our problems we don't mind. At least he should listen to us.' The Chancellor was perplexed. 'Why don't you see the people?' he asked the VC. 'They always come up with unreasonable demands. It's best to avoid them,' the VC answered by way of rationalisation. 'Moreover, if you keep them at a distance they

Contd.

Contd.

behave themselves, otherwise they agitate,' he opined. To explain the meaning of interpersonal relations, the Chancellor himself met the divergent groups and listened to their grievances. This was a shocking lesson to the VC who had just learned that using emotional intelligence helps in running the university smoothly.

Unbelievable, but true, is the fact that managers who fail are almost always high in expertise and IQ. Their fatal weakness in each case is their emotional intelligence, that is, arrogance, over-reliance on brainpower, inability to adapt to the occasionally disorienting shifts in their field and disdain for close collaboration or teamwork. An analysis of successful and failed managers reveals that those who failed lacked in emotional intelligence competencies and this, despite their strengths in technical and academic abilities. In the fast-changing modern world of mergers, acquisitions and coalitions, with new technologies, laws and rules, the lack of emotional intelligence in such an unstable environment means certain failure. Organisations, and the people manning them, need to sit up and acquire emotional intelligence. Our learned VC will also do well if he learns to develop his EQ.

☞ Definitions of EQ

Robert Cooper (1996): Emotional intelligence is the ability to sense, understand and effectively apply the power of and acumen of emotions as a source of human energy, information, trust, creativity and influence.

Reuven Bar-On (1997): Emotional intelligence reflects one's ability to deal with daily environment challenges and helps predict one's success in life, including professional and personal pursuits. *(Bar-On had coined the term EQ, i.e., emotional quotient, in 1985.)*

J. Mayer and P. Salovey (1997): Emotional intelligence is the ability to perceive emotions, to access and generate emotions so as to assist thought, to understand emotions and emotional knowledge, and to reflectively regulate emotions so as to promote emotional and intellectual growth.

Contd.

Contd.

Daniel Goleman (1998): Emotional intelligence is the capacity for recognising our own feelings and those of others, for motivating ourselves, and for managing emotions well in ourselves and in our relationships. Emotional intelligence describes abilities distinct from, but complementary to, academic intelligence or the purely cognitive capacities measured by IQ.

J. Freedman (1998): Emotional intelligence is a way of recognizing, understanding and choosing how we think, feel and act. It shapes our interaction with others and our understanding of ourselves. It defines how and what we learn, it allows us to set priorities, it determines the majority of our daily actions.

Dalip Singh (2003): Emotional intelligence is the ability of an individual to appropriately and successfully respond to a vast variety of emotional stimuli being elicited from the inner self and immediate environment. Emotional intelligence constitutes three psychological dimensions: emotional sensitivity, emotional maturity and emotional competency, which motivate an individual to recognise truthfully, interpret honestly and handle tactfully the dynamics of human behaviour.

Jitendra Mohan (2003): Emotional intelligence is a positive combination of a deep insight into one's emotional and cognitive capacities and a charming flair of communication, empathy and motivation, leading to personal optimism, inter-personal confluence and organizational excellence.

Mala Kapadia (2004): Emotional intelligence from Vedic psychology perspective can be described as transformation of mind, body and spirit to realise our true potential for the universal well being and abundance of joy.

Vinod Sanwal (2004): Emotional intelligence is the awareness of use of emotions and their utilization within the parameters of individual cognitive styles to cope with situations and problems.

N.K. Chadha (2005): All intelligence have an emotional base. Using your emotions as a source of energy to accomplish the self-defined goals is what emotional intelligence consists of.

Parmananda Chabungbam (2005): EI [or EQ] is the ability of a person to control impulses and persist in the face of frustration.

Contd.

Contd.

> **Ravi Bangar (2005):** Emotional intelligence is the capacity to create optimal results in your relationships with yourself and others.
> **Samira Malekar (2005):** Emotional intelligence is a set of factors which involve awareness of self and managing emotions, developing oneself through the power of empathy and motivation and building strong relationship with people.
> **Madhumati Singh (2006):** Emotional intelligence is the ability and freedom to grow from mistrust to trust, self-doubt to self-empowerment, following to leading, incompetence to competence, isolation to synergy and despair to hope.

How Do You Acquire Your EQ?

Your emotional makeup is the product of your learning experiences. Emotional competencies, abilities and concepts are learned through role models, i.e., teachers, parents, celluloid heroes and so on. You learn emotional intelligence through the social learning process. At no point of time in your life does someone tell you how to understand yourself and others, or how to handle interpersonal relations. This is something every one of you is expected to learn on your own and use these concepts in personal and professional life. Knowledge of emotional intelligence is taken for granted in society without realising that you were never formally exposed to such concepts. To put it simply, no formal education or knowledge is imparted to teach these concepts, abilities or competencies. This has created a strange situation: when you grow up in society or the workplace, family and others expect you to have adequate and appropriate knowledge of these concepts. Another problem is that there is a widespread belief in developing societies that intelligence has to do with thinking, analysing, remembering, comparing, applying, appearing for exams, obtaining high marks, and so on. These qualities, it is argued, lead to top positions, lucrative pay packages, palatial houses, imported cars, security, success and holidays. Consequently, people work hard to develop their IQ and ignore their EQ. Almost all over the world, most children spend 10 to 15 years of their life learning to develop their academic skills. In the process, emotions are either completely or largely ignored and there is no effort to inculcate them in our personal and professional life. It is unfortunate that we make no planned or conscious effort to impart emotional skills to our future generations. The average person is using the outdated technique of 'trial and error' to solve emotional problems. Many of you still believe that your EQ is something you will anyway learn with time and there is no urgent need to acquire it right away.

There appears to be a dichotomy between the head and the heart. While delivering a keynote address on EQ at a workshop, I was taken aback when one of the participants, a CEO of a large private sector firm, asked, 'Now when most of us are over 40 years in age, and have reached top positions in the workplace, we are suddenly told about concepts like how to handle yourself, your bosses, your subordinates and how to improve interpersonal relations. We are being asked to master competencies, personal traits or a set of habits for effective and superior job performance. Why is it that management experts find these concepts to be of utmost importance and every workshop has detailed lectures on them?' Others joined him by saying that in schools and colleges, they were taught various subjects like history, political science, mathematics, chemistry, economics and geography. And now they were being told that knowledge of these academic subjects was not adequate and that they should have knowledge of psychological skills to handle ticklish circumstances in life. Why were these psychological skills not introduced to them at an early stage if these were so important for personality development? And suddenly at this late stage in life, experts were teaching them how to handle their boss, their spouse, their neighbour or even themselves. They were being educated on how to control anger, frustration, anxieties, stress and burnout. Others lamented that they learned these competencies through informal sources and experimented on them in their own way.

My answer to all these issues was that what they 'felt' was right and that these psychological skills should have been taught in our educational institutions in the early stages of life. But unfortunately, in all developing countries, the emphasis even today is on academic factors (read IQ) rather than emotional factors (read EQ).

> Our education system gives stress on IQ and not on EQ. We are expected to learn EQ from our parents, peer group or other role models.

With the passage of time, we have realised that emotional factors are as important as academic factors and, in most cases, more important. To another query as to what lessons would I prefer to teach my child, my answer was that I would teach my child only one lesson—to be emotionally literate. That is the skill the child will need in order to overcome stress, anxiety, frustration, disappointment, anger, hurt and despair. I would teach my child that difficult situations in life help to improve our self-esteem, courage and self-reliance, and enable us to handle life on our own terms.

My contention is that emotional intelligence is a right mixture of 'The Head' and 'The Heart', as shown in Figure 1.3.

Do we really believe in the process defined above? The answer is a big 'NO'. In most societies, culturally, we are taught to think of emotion as an intellectual response rather than an emotional response. You have been taught not to trust your emotions because emotions distort the accurate information supplied by the brain. Even the term 'emotional' often signifies a weak personality, one who is out of control or even childish and foolish at times. In fact, you have learned to mould your entire self-image around your

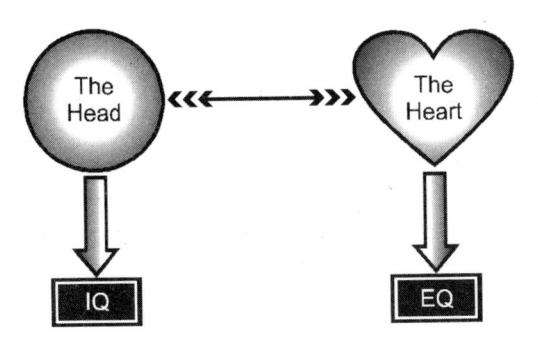

FIGURE 1.3: The Individual

intellect. Society tells you that academic intelligence is the means to get ahead and completely ignores the fact that human beings are not meant to be just think tanks. You have been told to value 'the head' and devalue 'the heart'. The fact is that instinctively, as an individual, you value the heart more than the head. You tend to suppress your emotions as a method of emotional management. That is what your parents, teachers and society have indirectly taught you, or perhaps you have learned it unconsciously. When you get into the habit of suppressing emotions in this way, you are holding back your emotions and trying to ensure that they do not reach the point of explosion. This can gradually become a source of abnormal behaviour and lead to other psychological problems. Job dissatisfaction, burnout, stress, inter-personal conflicts with seniors, colleagues or subordinates, frustration, anger and anxiety, are just a few factors that affect the productivity of oneself, of others and of organisations. An increase in the number of such instances has made management conscious that employees have to learn, or be taught, different methods of managing their emotions and expressing themselves in order to attain job satisfaction and productivity. Let us examine another case to further investigate this issue.

☞ Making Life's Dreams Come True

Let us meet a young wife-cum-working executive from Singapore, who tells us how to eliminate frustration and improve performance in life. 'In my career as a banker, I have come across people with varying degrees of IQ, varying aptitudes and academic achievements. When I dissect the background of successful and unsuccessful people in various fields, I have felt that most of the time it is not the academically intelligent people who can claim to be "successful". On the other hand and contrary to the general belief, the people who seem to succeed more are the ones who are emotionally intelligent. In my profession, it is mutual respect and the trust of a client that matters. And you do not learn these skills in classrooms.

Contd.

Contd.

'When I judge myself on the same criteria, I see that life has been quite stressful right from childhood. I encountered emotional upheavals that are normally not faced by other ordinary mortals in day-to-day living. Most of us encounter tough situations in life and I have also had a fair share of them. The most difficult of the experiences made me a more emotionally stable and mentally clear person, and I came out of each uncomfortable experience as a more positive person, better equipped to face the more difficult problems of life. After every problem I often whispered to myself, "Have perseverance, stay motivated, the worse is yet to come and there shall never be any problem which I will not be equipped with to handle." There were the genuine problems of life which otherwise would have broken a normal person to pieces, but I had learned the emotional skills to survive and move on.

'I feel it is the emotional stability in me, a positive way of responding to people, a calm approach to life, a practical and realistic approach to handling day-to-day problems, faith in the basic goodness of human beings, understanding the idiosyncratic variations in human behaviour, which have made me a "successful" woman. Maybe I can call myself a "happy and contended person". And, yes, I am "successful", because when I see in retrospect and recall my dreams as a young girl, I find that I have been able to substantially achieve whatever I had felt was most important to me. I do not claim that my marriage is a fountain of eternal love, but it is definitely near to that. My family depends on me even for small needs, and I enjoy it. Success is a very relative term. It varies from person to person. I apply a simple emotional tool to keep myself happy. No matter what I do, I should do it to the best of my capabilities and in a fashion that makes me, and the people around me, comfortable.

'I manage my personal relations responsibly. While carrying out my duties at my workplace or at home, one thing that mattered to me most was to create harmony in the environment I work in, with the people around, whether they are my juniors, seniors or at the same level. I have tried to be at ease with myself while making extra efforts not to create problems for people with whom I interact. Creating harmony does not mean bowing to the wishes of others.

Contd.

Contd.

> In fact, it is an understanding of the other person's perspective, giving him/her due respect and communicating in the ways they best appreciate. Even after having abundance of joy and contentment in life, I feel that am capable of doing much more and always vive for fresh responsibility and opportunity. For, life is too precious and short and making your life's dreams come true within a limited lifetime cycle is a challenge which we all need to master.'

EQ Helps in Professional Success

A young executive of a large firm said, 'I have a master's degree in accounting. When I went to work for this firm, I thought my problems were going to be accounting problems. But they are not. They are people's problems.' This new approach to understanding people through analysing and understanding behaviour is the order of the day.

In recent times, we find a resurgence of interest in the 'why', 'how' and 'what' of our behaviour. Let us now see what determines professional success. Is it the intelligence or skills you possess, or is it something else? Perhaps, it is a combination of both. Exponents of emotional intelligence are of the view that your emotional make-up largely determines your professional success. EQ is at least as much a determinant of how far you will succeed, personally and professionally. It is fascinating to see how people with high IQ fail and those with lower intellectual endowment are a runaway success in their professional lives. There are innumerable such examples in business, politics, academics and administration. What are the ramifications of EQ for the professional? Clearly, emotional intelligence is the key determinant of success in the workplace. Even more significant is the basis on which you must form your own moral compass, both in the workplace and elsewhere. It is increasingly being recognised that EQ can be applied to the

> Your emotional make-up largely determines your professional success.

organisation's unique needs. Employees can learn the principles of EQ to become better team players, be more creative in their work and increase overall productivity. This can be achieved by learning powerful techniques to integrate and utilise the principles of applied emotional intelligence at the workplace. For instance, learning how to successfully remove obstacles, surmount blocks, resolve conflicts and deal with any issue that may have prevented you from accomplishing your managerial objectives, are skills that can be learned.

EQ can be instrumental in achieving success in many areas of professional life and also helps achieve organisational development. Psychologists have concluded that in the current fast changing corporate environment, you need more than just brains to run your business. They argue that leaders in business must make contact with their emotions and feelings for effective decision-making and problem solving. EQ can help in increasing productivity, speeding up adaptation to change, developing leadership skills, stimulating creativity and cooperation, responding effectively to competition, encouraging innovative thinking and improving retention of key employees. It can also help create an enthusiastic work environment, improve the way employees feel about themselves and how they relate to others, reduce stress levels and resolve emotional issues, improve health and well-being, improve relationships, heighten success, and enable employees to experience greater fulfilment. In work situations, EQ can facilitate in resolving past issues, help employees attain emotional power, enable them to resolve external and internal conflicts, enable them to accomplish their goals at all levels—physical, mental, emotional and spiritual and improve their mental abilities such as memory, clarity of thinking and decision-making or coordinating the work of their subordinates.

> In the corporate world, IQ gets you hired, but EQ gets you promoted.

In a formal meeting, for example, do you observe the subtle signs that indicate how others in the meeting react to what has been said? Do you pay as much attention to the subtle signs of non-verbal communication as to

> You need more than just brains to run your business.

what is actually being said? If you can read these signs you can know when people are clear and congruent, and when they are uncertain or unsure. Observing how others respond emotionally guides managers and supervisors in conducting a meeting effectively.

In the corporate world, IQ gets you hired, but EQ gets you promoted—or fired. There is an example of a manager who was asked to rank the top performers working with him. The results showed that they were not necessarily those with the highest IQs; they were those whose e-mails got answered. Workers who are good collaborators and popular with their colleagues are more likely to get the cooperation they need to achieve their goals than the socially awkward, lone geniuses.

Who are the persons most likely to get promoted? They are the persons whose emotional intelligence matches that of their employer as well as of their boss. Understanding and fulfilling the values and expectations of your organisation and your boss is also a key emotional skill. This can be an important indicator whether you will move up or down in the hierarchical ladder of the organisation. Do you position yourself as an integral part of the organisation and place emphasis on its core values such as personal satisfaction, quality, environment and shareholder satisfaction?

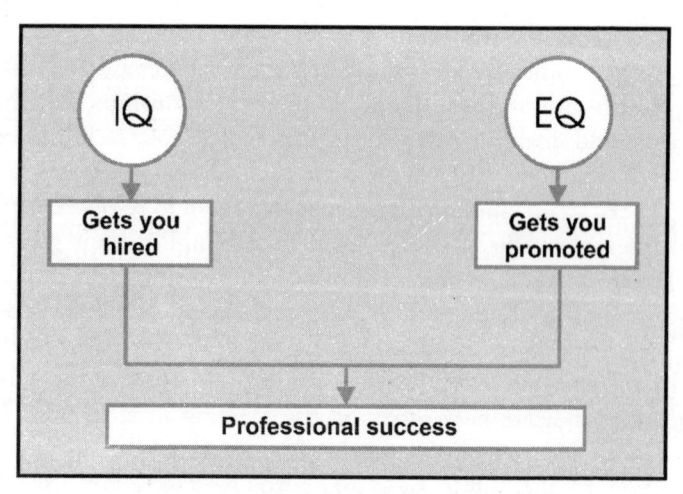

FIGURE 1.4: EQ Gets You Promoted!

Also, is the organisation making every effort to propagate this message? As an employee, you should know the answers to these questions. Ask yourself the question: 'Why did I choose this job?' Check out the criteria that are hidden in your answer. Is the work environment stimulating? Do you enjoy your job? Or do you do it for the money? Do you perceive it as a challenge, or as an opportunity to learn? If an employee does not fit into the company culture, he/she will have to face the consequences sooner or later.

Certainly, getting hired may be difficult. But what happens afterwards? Do you focus on getting a job or are you looking for a job for the rest of your life? How do you know whether you will fit into the company that seems attractive at first sight? This should not be a rational decision; let your emotions speak! 'Know thyself' is one of the maxims of emotional intelligence. EQ experts have interviewed managers and have concluded that successful people know the answers to the following questions. 'What is your vision for the future of your organisation? What will the world be like in the next, say, 20 years? What is your mission or goal in life? What is important for you at the workplace?' Emotionally intelligent people not only know their own answers, but also those of the company they work for. Knowing the answers helps them find out if they are compatible with the company they are working for. But how many people really do have a clear vision and mission of the organisation they work for, or of a personal goal for themselves? At this stage you may like to introspect and find the answers yourself.

If you try to find happiness in your work you stand a better chance of getting promoted. Find a company that is compatible with your vision, mission and values, and actually puts them into practice. This kind of work environment will be really stimulating. If there are some differences between you and the company, try to sort them out with the management. Keeping silent will only complicate matters in the long run. In commercial jobs, the ability to put yourself in another's shoes, as well as your capacity to understand the other person's behaviour, are essential emotional skills. By using EQ, managers can increase their awareness of emotional skills and understand what their company, their boss and their clients expect from them. If you fail to do so, which many of you may be doing consciously or unconsciously, the chances of losing your job would look bright.

Who are the persons most likely to be promoted, and what emotional skills should they possess? To answer these questions, we will study a few examples that will tell us that emotional factors play a significant role in attaining success at work. For example, how do people make decisions when confronted with failure or setbacks? Optimism is the emotional skill that helps in such situations. Optimists tend to make specific, temporary, external decisions while pessimists make global, permanent, internal decisions. It has been found that those insurance salespersons who were optimists, sold more insurance policies than did pessimists. It is clear that optimism makes such a difference in business and in life. Each rejection faced by a salesperson is a small defeat. The emotional reaction to such a defeat is crucial to the salesperson's ability to marshal up enough motivation to continue. As rejections mount, morale can deteriorate, making it increasingly difficult for the person to make the next sales call. Pessimists find such rejections especially hard to accept for they may interpret them to mean: 'I'm a failure at this; I'll never make a sale', an interpretation that is bound to trigger apathy and defeatism, frustration and depression. Optimists, on the other hand, are likely to tell themselves, 'I'm using the wrong approach,' or 'that last person was just in a bad mood'. By not blaming themselves but perceiving something else in the situation as being responsible for failure, they can adopt a new approach in the next sales call. While the pessimist's attitude may lead to despair, the optimist's spawns hope.

The skills required for handling stress is another important aspect of emotional intelligence that is related to success. The ability to successfully handle stress results in net profits. Yet another emotional skill is the management of emotions. Emotional intelligence has as much to do with knowing when and how to express emotion, as it does with controlling it. Most successful persons are warmer, more outgoing, emotionally expressive and sociable. Additionally, empathy is a particularly important aspect of emotional intelligence that also contributes to occupational success. People who were best at identifying others' emotions were more successful in their work as well as in their social lives. The lack of emotional self-control prevents you from moving up the hierarchy. You will find that more than half the people who work for you lack the motivation to keep learning and improving on the job. They are not able to work cooperatively with fellow employees, and do not have enough self-discipline in their work habits. More and more employers are complaining about the lack of emotional skills in new hires. Too many young people cannot take criticism: they get defensive or hostile when others make suggestions or give them feedback, which they construe as a personal attack. But this problem is not with the new generation alone; it is true for some seasoned managers as well. Many of them exhibit a lack of emotional intelligence.

Readers may note that the word 'success' has been used to define EQ. But what is 'success'? Is it to reach top positions in the workplace? Is it being rich and wealthy? Is it being powerful, dominating or influential? Is it occupying senior positions in bureaucracy? Or, is it something else? Should we conclude that people who could not reach the 'top' have failed in their professional or personal life and be designated as 'unsuccessful'? It is time to get closer to the meaning of 'success' to avoid misleading conclusions. You will agree that success cannot be defined only as being at the top position in an organisation or achieving a smooth career growth. Success may have different meanings for different people. For some, having a satisfying job or personal life may be an indication of success. Leading a healthy and happy married life may be a determinant of success for others. For yet another set of people, success may mean reaching the top position. Hence, tangible achievements alone may not be indicators of success in life. Non-tangible achievements can also be termed as successful. But how do you measure and quantify these? It therefore becomes imperative to know what we mean by 'success' in personal and professional life. Is there a standard definition for 'success'? Synonyms for the word 'successful' include flourishing, thriving, prospering, booming, growing, mushrooming, fruitful, lucrative and advancing. There are many definitions for the word 'success', depending upon the individual. By the way, are *you* clear on what success means to you? It must be remembered that succeeding is not like winning a 'lottery'; it is like a project that takes planning, research and implementation. Doctors, lawyers, engineers and other professionals do not accomplish their vocations overnight. The best athletes work out diligently every day to become the best. And successful entrepreneurs do not make it overnight either. It is true that you usually hear about successful people only after they have made it big, but they have worked at it behind the scenes for years, struggling and learning from their failures, until they finally achieve success (their individual goals)! While success *could* happen quickly for you, it usually does not. I believe that success is when preparation meets opportunity. On a positive note, it can be a fun and exciting learning process and experience for those who are willing to enjoy the journey.

What is Success?

Is it exams passed, competitions cleared, percentage of marks, earning fat salary, top positions in workplace, being rich, powerful, dominating, being influential
Or
Is success something else?

You may have encountered many 'rising stars' that have burned out. It has been observed that executives most often failed because of an interpersonal shortcoming, and not because of any technical inability. Many fatal flaws are related to classic emotional failings, such as poor working relations, authoritarianism or excessive ambition and conflict with top management. EQ has given a new dimension to business and industry. In the marketing world, it is increasingly being realised that it is the customer or client who is at the centre-stage. Customers are telling businesses, 'We do not care if every member of your staff graduated with honours from Harvard, Stanford, Mumbai or Delhi. We will go where we are understood and treated with respect.' Such a response is forcing management institutes to rework and redesign their conventional and stereotyped course curriculum that has already outlived its practical utility.

Some Myths about EQ

There are certain widespread myths about emotional intelligence, and it is important to dispel the most common ones.

First, emotional intelligence does not mean merely 'being nice'. At strategic moments such intelligence may in fact demand 'not being nice' and, instead, bluntly confronting someone with an uncomfortable but consequential truth they may have been avoiding.

Second, emotional intelligence does not mean giving free rein to feeling, 'letting it all hang out'. Rather, it involves managing feelings so that these are expressed appropriately and effectively, enabling people to work together smoothly towards common goals.

Third, women are not necessarily 'smarter' than men when it comes to emotional intelligence, nor are men 'superior' to women. Each one has a personal profile of strengths and weaknesses in these capacities. For instance, some may be highly empathic but lack certain abilities to handle distress; some may be quite aware of the subtlest shift in another's moods, yet be inept socially. However, it is also true that men and women, as groups, tend to have a shared, gender-specific profile of strengths and weaknesses. An analysis of emotional intelligence in thousands of men and women revealed that women, on an average, were more aware of their emotions, showed more empathy and were more adept interpersonally. Men, on the other hand, were more self-confident

EQ is Not—
- Fixed genetically
- Being nice or good all the time
- To give free rein to feelings
- Something that develops in early childhood
- Having gender differences
- Supporting average IQ persons

and optimistic, adapted more easily and handled stress better. In general, there are far more similarities than differences. Some men are as empathic as the most interpersonally sensitive women, while some women are able to withstand stress as much as the most emotionally resilient men. Indeed, as far as the overall ratings for men and women are concerned, their strengths and weaknesses average out, so that there are no sex differences in total emotional intelligence.

Finally, the level of emotional intelligence is not fixed genetically, nor does it develop only in early childhood. Unlike IQ, which does not change much after adolescence, emotional intelligence is largely learned and continues to develop throughout life; as you learn from your experiences, your EQ also keeps growing.

2

Emotional Intelligence and Your Personality

> Everything that irritates us about others can lead us to an understanding of ourselves.
> —*Carl Jung*

Your emotional intelligence, also known as EQ, reflects your personality. To understand how your EQ makes or mars your personality development, let us look at some crucial issues.

THE RELATIONSHIP BETWEEN EQ AND IQ

It is very important to understand that EQ is not the opposite of IQ, it is not the triumph of heart over head—it is the unique interaction of both. The relationship between emotions and rational intelligence is a complex one. Instead of accepting the historic dichotomy between reason and emotion, between academic basics and emotional basics, it is important to appreciate how

> IQ is a measure of intelligence quotient whereas EQ is a measure of emotional quotient.

these interact. Through conscious effort, emotional responses can be regulated and used appropriately; it is when such awareness is lacking that emotional reactions override rational thought.

Traditionally, psychologists measure intelligence through various intelligence quotient (IQ) tests. The formula used for IQ tests is simple and elegant. It compares an individual's 'chronological age' with his/her 'mental age'. For example, if a person's mental age

> **The IQ Formula**
> IQ = MA/CA × 100
> (Intelligence Quotient = Mental Age divided by Chronological Age × 100)

is 30 and chronological age is 20, then his/her IQ is 150. The average intelligence of the majority of people is 100, that is, their mental age equals their chronological age (the actual age). IQ tests are used in a variety of settings, including schools, armed forces and businesses, with the aim of determining how well a person is able to learn. Similarly, we can determine EQ by using scientific psychological tests that have been developed to measure emotional intelligence. (See Chapter 7)

EQ is not the opposite of IQ. Some people have high EQ as well as IQ, while others are low on either. Researchers have been making efforts to understand how they complement one another; how a person's ability to handle stress, for instance, affects his/her ability to concentrate and put his/her intelligence to use. Some people can handle anger well but cannot handle fear. Others are incapable of reacting to joy. Therefore, each emotion needs to be viewed differently. IQ is a measure of intelligence quotient whereas EQ is a measure of emotional quotient. It is now widely believed that emotions, rather than IQ, may be the true measure of human intelligence. Therefore, scientists are shifting their focus from the hardware of the brain to the software of the mind. We should keep in mind that cognitive (IQ) and non-cognitive (EQ) abilities are closely related. In fact, research suggests that emotional and social skills help improve cognitive functioning.

Emphasising EQ does not mean de-emphasising IQ. The latter is not less relevant for success in job performance or life than the former. The fact remains that one needs a relatively high level of IQ merely to get admitted to a science or engineering course. However, once you are admitted, how you compare with your peers has less to do with IQ differences and more to do with emotional factors, or EQ. To put it in another way, if you're a scientist, you probably needed an IQ of 120 or so, simply to get a doctorate and a job. But then it is more important to be able to persist in the face of difficulty and to get along well with colleagues and subordinates than it is to have an extra 10 or 15 points of IQ. The same is true in many other occupations and professions. However, this need not lead us to the erroneous conclusion that low academic scorers with high EQ have a better chance of being successful. Our premise is that IQ, by itself, is not a very good predictor of job performance. There are other factors that add to overall personality development and satisfying performance at work. These 'other' factors relate to behaviour, moods and emotions, and are now broadly coined as emotional factors. This premise has led to the propagation of the concept of emotional quotient (EQ). For example, if you are a first class graduate or gold medallist in engineering or science, it may not automatically mean that you will have smooth relations with your spouse, or you will be liked by your boss or subordinates, or you will handle emotional upsets effectively. It may not be out of place to say that most high-IQ persons tend to get derailed from the emotional or social path.

WHERE DO EMOTIONS COME FROM?

Human beings are psychologically very complex. The human mind is able to reason, remember, learn and form concepts or ideas, as well as direct actions, towards specific goals. In other words, human beings are not only motivated by reason and intelligence, but are also subject to passions, desires, and a range of other feelings which can motivate them strongly—often in a direction different from that of reason. These feelings are called emotions. Some psychologists have compared them to the mainspring (or battery) of a watch. Just as the hands of a watch would be motionless without the mainspring or battery, so would human beings be listless and accomplish little or nothing if there were no emotions to motivate them.

| EQ + IQ = Intelligence |

There is another way of describing emotions. There are certain things that you consider pleasant, and others that you view as unpleasant. Certain things appeal to you, while some others repel you. The basis for deciding what is pleasant or unpleasant, what is appealing or objectionable, is quite uncertain. Why, for instance, are some people afraid of snakes, spiders and cockroaches, while others show no fear of them at all? One explanation could be that such fear is a reflex conditioned by an experience early in life. But fear can also be expressed for the unknown, without any prior conditioning. For example, you may suddenly come upon an animal by chance, and having never seen one before, be instantly afraid of it.

Neuroscientists and evolutionists have done brilliant work to explain the reasons underlying some of the most unreasonable behaviour. In the past decade or so, scientists have learned enough about the human brain to make judgements about where emotion arises and why it is necessary. Primitive emotional responses hold the key to survival: in fear the blood flows in the larger muscles, making it easier to run; in surprise the eyebrows rise, allowing the eyes to widen their view and gather in more information about an unexpected event; in disgust the face and the nostrils wrinkle up. Every emotion is an impulse which makes you cry, laugh, run, scared, and so on.

> Human beings operate from two minds, the emotional mind and the rational mind.

The latest research in neurobiology has shown that human beings operate from two minds: the emotional mind and the rational mind. The harmony between the two minds is what constitutes emotional intelligence and is the key to a richer and more fulfilling life, as shown in Figure 2.1.

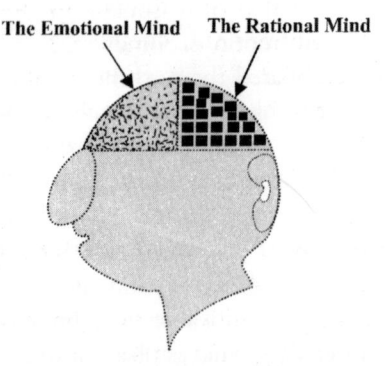

FIGURE 2.1: The Human Mind

The *emotional mind* is the source of basic emotions: anger, sadness, fear, lust, surprise, disgust, and so on. Earlier species, including humans, operated exclusively from the emotional mind—the old sub-cortical limbic system lying beneath the grey matter.

The *rational mind* is centred in the neo-cortex, the outer part of the brain, and allows humans to plan, learn and remember. Historically, the subtler part of the brain, or the neo-cortex, developed about a million years ago.

Research done in the early 1990s reveals that messages from the senses are, in fact, registered by the brain in emotional memory, the amygdala, where emotions are stored. This means that emotional intelligence actually contributes to rational intelligence. It is your emotional brain that analyses emotional decisions such as who you should marry, make friends with, or worst, show enmity towards. It is now believed that your emotions take precedence over your thoughts in making decisions, because the rational mind takes a little longer to register and respond than the emotional mind. The first impulse in a situation arises in the heart, not in the head. In an emotional reaction, there is an extended appraisal of the situation, though thoughts also play a key role in determining what emotions will be aroused. Once an appraisal is made by the brain that 'that taxi driver is cheating me' or 'this baby is adorable', an appropriate emotional response follows. More complicated emotions, such as embarrassment or apprehension, follow this slower route and are expressed after a few seconds or minutes; they follow from thoughts. But the rational mind normally does not decide what emotions you 'should' have. Instead, it is your feelings that typically come to you as a *fait accompli*. What the rational mind can ordinarily do is to control the course of these reactions. For example, you do not decide when to be mad, sad, angry or depressed. It is the situation that decides how you react and behave.

> There really are no negative or positive emotions.

There really are no positive or negative emotions. Emotion is emotion, and it serves some purpose. Emotion is necessary for survival or for protecting yourself; it leads to action that prevents or minimises perceived loss or pain. If it were not for the experience of pain, you would probably have chewed your fingers off by now! It is emotion that drives you to act in ways that help you from a basic survival standpoint. It would therefore be incorrect to define emotional states such as peace, joy, compassion and happiness as 'positive emotions', or anger, hate, jealousy and anxiety as 'negative emotions'. Emotion is largely an automatic response determined by the way you set yourself up to respond and react to the world. Hence, emotions are reactions to specific situations and cannot be termed as positive or negative. It is therefore advisable to be intelligent about your emotions.

CONSEQUENCES OF LOW AND HIGH EQ

Research and experience clearly demonstrate that while some aspects of your personality are fixed, you may, however, choose the way you want to react to them. In other words, you do not be able to choose your characteristics or many of the events in your life, but you can choose how to react to them. This conclusion may be unpalatable to some, but inescapable nonetheless; you are responsible for your thoughts, emotions and consequential actions. Your emotional response, as is generally believed, is not your destiny but your own conscious decision. How you use your emotions to tackle day-to-day problems is what reflects the amount of EQ you have. Since EQ is important, it is necessary to know the consequences of having a low or high EQ.

Consequence of low EQ is the feeling of general unhappiness. If what you can't deal with upsets easily, and if you are uncomfortable with yourself, you need to check your EQ. The benefits of being aware of how you feel from an interpersonal point of view will not be available to you if your EQ is on the lower side. You may not be able to choose a friend who is best suited to you because you are not aware of your own inner emotions. If your EQ is not high, it is likely that you will choose a friend who is not well suited to you. You may even choose as friend a person who makes logical sense but who just cannot make you feel 'good'. The cost of this may be very high. Eventually, you may find excuses to end such a friendship.

Consequence of high EQ is the feeling of general happiness. When you have a high EQ, you are more likely to recognise the source of your emotions, and have the confidence to take appropriate actions, thus increasing long-term happiness. You will set your own standards by closely examining your own values and beliefs. You will lead your life according to your own terms, rather than be governed by society's norms. Finally, the higher your EQ, the more you will assume responsibility for your own happiness, and depend less on society. Research on EQ has revealed that people high on EQ are happier, healthier and more successful in their relationships. They strike a balance between emotion and reason, are aware of their own feelings, are empathic and compassionate towards others and also show signs of high self-esteem. Table 2.1 explains some consequences of high and low EQ:

TABLE 2.1: Consequences of Levels of EQ

Low EQ		High EQ	
Unhappiness	Failure	Happiness	Appreciation
Frustration	Dejection	Satisfaction	Freedom
Emptiness	Anger	Peace	Desire
Bitterness	Dependence	Awareness	Contentment
Depression	Loneliness	Self-esteem	Elation
Instability	Stress	Balance	Motivation

We may conclude by saying that emotional intelligence is the capacity to create positive outcomes in your relationships with others and with yourself. Positive outcomes include joy, optimism, and success in work, school, and life. Increasing emotional intelligence (EQ) has been correlated with better results in leadership, sales, academic performance, marriage, friendships, and health. Learning some emotional skills such as expressing emotions, identifying and labelling emotions, assessing the intensity of emotions, managing emotions, delaying gratification, controlling impulses, reducing stress and knowing the difference between emotions and actions can make you a star performer.

☞ The Energetic CEO Who Failed

This is the case of a CEO of a large public sector company, with 30 years of experience and an IQ of 200. But his EQ seems to be low. He spent the greater part of the day at his desk, crunching figures in a race against himself and rarely succeeded in going home early. Normally, he worked for more than 18 hours a day and took great 'pride' in doing so. He spent much of his energy complaining to his colleagues, 'My chairman has an IQ of 90. My chairman has no idea what I do! Moreover my subordinates never extend the support I need to get things done right.' Is all this true? Is it unjust? The CEO thought so, and so did his blood pressure. What he had not told his colleagues was that his own work was unimpressive in ways that really mattered. He was oblivious of the fact that he was a troubleshooter who got so bogged down in minute details that he rarely saw the larger picture. He also had not noticed his chairman's grimace when he handed him unnecessarily technical and complex reports that were a painful struggle to decipher. He valued rules, regulations, instructions, laws, acts, reports, etc. but he had not heard of interpersonal relations. It had not occurred to him that everyone perceived him as a big bore and tried to avoid him. He could not see why he should spend any time worrying about other people's emotions. After all, he had never got any sympathy from them when, year after year, he was neglected for promotion. The CEO had not learned the simple lesson that intellect alone could not help him navigate the dynamic political, administrative and psychological situations of an office full of people, each with a different set of needs and desires. He lacked empathy to guess what his boss wants and learn which projects really carry the most corporate weight, to realise a subordinate's tension and not overload him or her with work, and to sense a client's dissatisfaction despite his or her protestations.

Were he to learn to raise his EQ, he would find his intellectual capacities expanded and emotional skills enhanced. He would feel more secure in his ability to perceive and respond to his own emotional needs and could therefore risk responding to the needs of others. In doing so, he would move ahead and be able to handle his chairman more effectively and in the process do something about his blood pressure also.

3

Can EQ be Developed?

> It is never too late to make changes in your life or help others do the same.

YES. EQ can be developed by upgrading your emotional skills. This widespread belief that EQ is entirely inherited is not quite correct. Emotional intelligence is not fixed at birth. Scientists have not yet discovered an 'emotional intelligence' gene. It is something you have learnt (or not learnt). EQ impacts you not only at work, but also outside the workplace. It affects how good you feel, how much you can achieve and the quality and richness of your relationships. It impacts parents as well as children. It impacts CEOs, managers and workers. What is important is that you can develop your EQ through a step-by-step process. Increasing EQ offers quick dividends and affects many areas of your life. People are becoming increasingly aware that the ability to feel is as vital to their well being as the ability to think. This feeling is now gaining ground worldwide. You need to understand the critical importance of your raw emotions, but often you do not know how to do so. How do you learn to master and make use of the often complex and confusing emotions? How do you raise your emotional intelligence? Human beings are not all created emotionally equal: all have widely differing natural temperaments.

> Your EQ is not fixed at birth. The same is not true of IQ, which is more or less static.

The way you act out, express yourself and utilise your emotions can be changed significantly. Unlike IQ, EQ can be significantly developed. Let us now see how we can do it.

Early Life Experiences

Emotional development starts early in life and closely related to child development. Healthy emotional development of children is vital to both their ability to learn, when young, and to their success and happiness as adults. Experience shows that the emotional development of children has by and large been neglected, especially in under-developed and developing countries. As a result, children often bear the brunt of emotionally unskilled individual parenting and rigid cultural and religious tradition. It would be worthwhile to examine the psychology of child development to understand emotional development.

Childhood is a unique window on time when a child's mental frame can actually be sculpted by parental example. EQ offers parents guidance in recognising and nurturing emotional intelligence in their children, both within the home and outside. Volatile behaviour, for example, is typical of 2-year-olds and is not aimed personally at anyone. What your toddler's actions reflect, first and foremost, is the struggle that accompanies his desire to decipher emotions. Academic Intelligence is certainly an asset and hailed as paramount, particularly in today's information age. But parents want their child to be happy as well as smart. Hence, a child's emotional education has to begin increasingly earlier and be more intense than ever. For instance, babies are even read to in the womb, and infant toys are designed for cerebral stimulation. While such methods may produce intelligent children, something else, which is just as important, may be overlooked. To excel in life, a child needs to master the art of emotional intelligence. Furthermore, it is believed that having a high IQ in today's world is not really discounted, but a high EQ is what is becoming increasingly popular. In many advanced countries, traditional education is increasingly tilted towards academic achievement, and as a result children may have to face a great deal of emotional pressure and frustration. In developing countries, the concept of emotional intelligence, which emphasises emotional education, has gained significance; it shows the way to break the IQ myth and move towards a multifaceted and balanced education.

EQ DEVELOPS WITH MATURITY

The process of developing EQ is not too difficult. Nevertheless, it is widely believed that it is not simple either, despite all the knowledge about emotional intelligence. In fact, according to latest scientific research, emotional intelligence may be even more important than IQ. The good news about emotional intelligence is that, unlike IQ, it can be improved throughout life. In a serendipitous fashion, life offers innumerable chances to tone your emotional competence. In the normal course of a lifetime, emotional intelligence tends to increase as you learn to be more aware of your emotions, to effectively handle distressing emotions, to listen and empathise; in short, as you become more mature your EQ increases. To a large extent, maturity itself describes this process of becoming more intelligent about your emotions and relationships. In a comparison of several hundred adults and adolescents, it has been found that adults across the board had higher EQ. An evaluation of the emotional intelligence of men and women of ages varying from the teens to the 50s, revealed small but steady and significant increases in their emotional intelligence with advancing age.

> Emotional intelligence develops with increasing age and experience, as a person progresses from childhood to adulthood.

Further, a peak was observed in the 40s age group. It was confirmed that emotional intelligence developed with increasing age and experience as a person progressed from childhood to adulthood. Additionally, it was seen that when it came to cultivating emotional competence, maturity remained an advantage; it may be slightly harder to actually 'teach young dogs new tricks'! Nevertheless, we may say that given the motivation, older workers are as good, or even better, than younger ones in mastering new levels of emotional intelligence. While women tend to be stronger in competencies based on empathy and social skills, men do better in those based on self-regulation. However, men and women could

> Men and women are equal in their ability to increase emotional intelligence.

improve to the same extent, regardless of where they started on a given competence.

A Case Study

How is emotional intelligence developed in organisations? This question is increasingly being asked by modern-day managers. Organisations do not only deal with materials, they also deal with people. The EQ of an organisation can be judged from the way it deals with issues of leadership, interpersonal relations, communication and relations with other organisations. How do employees counter stressful and conflicting situations? How do they handle frustrations? The trust and credibility of a manager and the organisation he or she is working with reflects its emotional intelligence level. Let us see how EQ was developed to improve work performance in a public sector hotel.

☞ EQ Improves Work Performance

Introduction
A public sector three star hotel in northern India was continuously incurring losses for the last five years. This was despite the fact that the city attracted a large number of Indian and foreign tourists. A quick diagnosis showed that the occupancy rate had fallen from 90 to 30 in five years, the profits were going down, poor maintenance was the order of the day, there was lack of coordination among various wings of the hotel, guest satisfaction was at an all time low, absenteeism among staff was vulnerably high, corruption was rampant and the morale of the staff had nose dived. Shockingly enough, the private sector hotels in the same town were doing thriving business. In January 2004, a new Executive Director (ED) was appointed by the Government. He had many challenges on hand without any indication of how to overcome them. When the new ED conducted his first meeting with the senior staff he concluded that 'there was no hope of survival of this hotel'. The de-motivated staff also nodded by saying, 'It's dead. It is only waiting for burial'.

Contd.

Contd.

The new ED struggled to bring in positive change in personnel and economic performance but could move only by inches in the first two months. To keep his faint hope alive to resurrect the hotel, he invited EQ experts to solve the problem and suggest changes.

EQ Intervention

The EQ expert team went around focusing on the trouble, its manifested causes, and solutions. It conducted 'focus group' discussions to bring home the genesis of the problem. The discussions included senior, middle and shop floor personnel singularly and jointly for four days. An EQ test was administered to know the current level of understanding of emotions of all concerned. The results showed psychological maladjustments in inter and intra personnel matters. With the active involvement of all opinion leaders, the 'trouble spots' were narrowed down. The consensus arrived at was to 'do something' to recover from the present crisis without identifying 'what it could be'. The EQ experts helped in identifying and labeling these areas as 'lack of emotional sensitivity, maturity and corresponding lack of knowledge of competencies required to be a winner'. These experts remained in constant touch with the management for a period of six months and imparted training in areas henceforth unheard of by the staff. Among other issues, the staff was given an overview of emotional intelligence, how it affects performance and whether it can be improved my measurable instruments or not. The intervention stressed the importance of emotions both for interfacing as a team, with employees, and with customers and others. The senior staff wanted one-to-one coaching which was provided. The ED was briefed about the projected performance appraisal of the senior managers and was advised to change/replace some of them if he also felt so. The EQ experts imparted training in emotional competencies to recover lost morale and motivation and increase productivity. Surprisingly for the EQ team, everyone in the organisation participated with vigor and responsibility as they had by now felt that the hotel might face closure in the times to come. The ED replaced four managers, transferred twice the number and said goodbye to one. The management team was advised to increase training schedules

Contd.

Contd.

> and make extensive efforts to raise quality standards and expectations of customers and employees.
>
> *Outcome*
> The six-month long intervention by the EQ experts resulted in positive and significant improvement. The quantifiable results showed that the coordination skills improved by 32.80%, accountability by 30.87% and sharing and exchanging information by 20.50%. The absenteeism rate dropped down from 40% to an unbelievable 5%. These changes were noticed by the hotel's customers and clients. They now felt that the hotel was passionate about their needs, and exhibited feelings of trust, respect and friendliness. Guest satisfaction on a ten point scale jumped to 9.2 from 3.2 earlier. The turnover increased, bringing the hotel out of the red, and its market share improved. These significant changes were the result of improved emotional skills of personnel at all levels, specially the ED who was trained to became a star performer and lead his team toward the promised goals. The EQ expert team was complimented by the management for helping them recognise, identify and appropriately use their emotional skills. They acknowledged that it had not only improved their work performance but also helped them improve personal relationships.

EMOTIONS CAN BE UNLEARNED

Emotions are learned habits, and therefore can be learned or unlearned. There is no gainsaying that an environment of distrust, manipulation, corruption, negative feelings and low morale can prove to be disastrous at the workplace. Moreover, the rapidly increasing incidence of violent crime, industrial strikes, marital strife, teenage drug abuse, low morale, a decline in national character and other ills can be attributed to the lack of EQ. Psychological research has demonstrated that it is possible to develop levels of emotional intelligence in such situations by asking people to unlearn bad emotional responses and equip them with the necessary emotional competence to deal with such situations. For instance, the ability to control anger or develop empathy is likely to be a better indicator of future success than the kind of academic intelligence put into practice by academicians throughout the world. Let us see the case of an engineer to understand this point.

☞ The Reticent Engineer

Consider the reticent engineer who does not venture out of his cubicle nor interacts with his colleagues. He feels that he and his computer are enough to handle all work-related problems. Why does he behave in this manner? His self-imposed isolation may be due to shyness, social ineptness, or in simply being unskilled in the art of teamwork. Whatever the specific cause of his isolation, he is the victim of a learned habit. He has not learned how to affiliate, coordinate or assimilate his emotions with that of his colleagues. Such a situation causes difficulties for him. However, with less effort and time he can unlearn what had been learned and cultivate a more effective habit. The unlearning and learning processes occur at the level of brain connections. As you acquire a habitual repertoire of thoughts and emotions, the neural connections that support this repertoire are strengthened, becoming dominant pathways for nerve impulses. Connections that are not used weaken or may even get lost, whereas those that are used over and over again grow increasingly strong. And the process of learning and unlearning goes on, with more and more practice.

Emotional skills can be viewed as a coordinated bundle of habits of what you think, feel and do, to complete a job. When such habits become dysfunctional, replacing them with more effective habits may require a lot of practice. The effective habit will eventually replace the old one as the automatic response in key situations. This kind of learning or 'rewriting', which is the test of your emotional skill, depends on how you automatically react at a crucial moment.

The reticent engineer can master the art of unlearning and learning, in such situations where he has a critical choice, to improve his emotional skills. He can either remain in his cubicle, working alone at his computer, or he can consult his co-workers who have valuable information and expertise. If he spontaneously steps out of his cubicle to approach a colleague, and does so effectively, it indicates that a new habit has been mastered.

Managers and employees who have the habit of learning and unlearning emotional reactions to situations are more successful than their counterparts who are merely technically qualified. They are better liked, more cooperative, more trusted, more resilient, intrinsically more motivated and optimistic. They are also adept at avoiding conflicts and at resolving them, when they do occur. They also know, for example, how to prevent conflicts from escalating. When the managers values emotions, so will the subordinates. Research confirms what commonsense would suggest: emotions are contagious. Thus, if the executive feels optimistic, confident, creative, flexible, tolerant, respectful and compassionate, employees down the hierarchy will tend to feel the same way as well. Research also indicates that the direction of emotional flow is top down as expected, since anyone in power by default, has more influence. Hence, it would be a good idea to unlearn those emotional reactions that cause trouble and instead learn those that make you feel happy.

Examples of EQ Development

Let us now see how development of EQ helps organisations achieve greater success. Increasingly, organisations are realising that encouraging emotional intelligence skills are a vital component of management philosophy. 'You don't compete with products alone anymore, but also how well you use your people,' said a manager. A vice president at a bank said, 'Emotional intelligence is the underlying premise for all management training. It's a refrain heard time and again.' The Consortium for Research on Emotional Intelligence in Organisations (2005) has enumerated several examples to illustrate how development of EQ contributes to the bottom line in any organisation. Based on data from a variety of sources, these examples can serve as valuable tools for HR practitioners and managers who need to develop EQ in their organisations and also in personal life. Some of the studies have been cited here to highlight how a developed EQ can help organisations in achieving their objectives.

1. Mort Meyerson, former chairman and CEO of Perot Systems, attempted to transform his organisation.

> We convened meetings of the top 100 people in the company and asked them a list of questions: How did they feel about the company culture? What was their evaluation of our top executives? What were their feelings about our customer relations? The answers were a laundry list of horrifying bad news. Our people were angry, frustrated, irritated and deeply unhappy. We set up teams to address these concerns and then reconvened the top 100 to ask them, again, how they felt. We got the same answers. We initiated a company-wide programme to teach them how to disagree with each other without tearing each other down. All our company leaders in the United States and Europe participated; and we extended it down into the ranks, so that today two-thirds of the company has been through the course. During these seminars, we identified people who were abusive. We coached them and took them through a personal re-invention process to show them new ways of leading. These were high-ranking company officials who had generated significant business, met or exceeded their financial goals, but simply mistreated their people. Not all of them could convert. Those who couldn't change were asked to leave. We gave them fair and extended compensation; we didn't strong-arm them out of the door; and we tried to keep communications open with them. We simply told them that this wasn't a company that was right for them. Earlier, we told people to leave their personal problems at home. Now we make it clear that personal issues are our issues as well. Not long ago, one of our sales executives had a child born with a hole in its heart. Through e-mail, we knew about the child within four hours of its birth. Within eight hours we had a specialist working with the infant. The child will now be able to lead a normal life. Our company made that happen because it was the right thing [to do]. It is not the only kind of things we should do but it does represent what we should be, the kind of feeling our company should create. On customer relations, our tone was often paternalistic, almost condescending. Customers felt like they were outgunned at every turn. Too often we made them feel incompetent or just plain stupid. You do better if your customer or your competitor doesn't feel taken advantage of. You do better, in fact, if your customer feels like your partner. We coached them in good customer relations. And our strategy worked and helped us in building an environment of emotional trust.

2. The communication strategy of Coca-Cola Corporation was ineffective in the marketing of its new product. 'New Coke' is probably one of the best-known marketing failures in the last 10 years. Before releasing the product, it had been tested in all possible ways. The test panels all agreed: 'New Coke tastes a lot

better than the old Coke', and Coca-Cola Corporation decided to launch New Coke as a replacement of the old product. Expectations were high, but after a couple of weeks it was observed that the sales figures dropped at an unprecedented rate. EQ experts were hired to analyse the problem and it was found that New Coke appealed to only about 10 per cent of the US population. How come? From a psychological point of view, the name 'New Coke' is directed toward a segment of customers who want something new from time to time. They are often known as the 'early adopters'. These customers differ from the rest of the population who prefer to buy products they are familiar with. When a new product is launched, the more conservative customers take longer to be convinced (the early adopters help to convince them). The problem facing Coca-Cola was that it could not afford such a long adaptation period. So the old product was re-launched as 'Classic Coke'. This time, the product appealed to 65 per cent of its old customer base. This did not come as a surprise to the EQ experts, since they had predicted that such a change would be against the psychological preferences of 30 per cent of the customers. Considering all these problems, it came as a surprise when another new product of the company called 'Cherry Coke' appealed to the US market. This new product was similar to an old-style soft drink, produced on a small scale by many drugstores in the 1950s. In fact, Coca-Cola copied a product that the customer was already familiar with and introduced some changes in it. Again, the product appealed to the 65 per cent of the population who essentially preferred similar products, but sought some changes from time to time. To complete the story, New Coke disappeared from the market about 18 months after it had been introduced.

3. A US-based organisation lost 25 per cent of all salespersons hired, during their first year, primarily due to poor performance. This represented a lost training and employment cost of about US $3 million per annum. The organisation decided to make EQ a prerequisite for recruitment. Semi-structured interviews were held as part of the total pre-employment screening process. This process, in effect, compared the applicant's scores against the real world model of sales success and classified applicants to 'fit' this model. Since the process was added to the overall employment screening process, attrition due to sales 'failure' decreased by over 80 per cent. Not only did this represent a significant saving in the huge lost personnel cost, it also improved the overall 'fit' between the person, the job and the organisational culture. The model served as a road map to guide the training content for new recruits, further 'optimising' them for success. Once these critical skills became known, training programmes were revised to include these areas. The results confirm the characteristics of the best-performing companies today. Some of these characteristics indicate that there is no substitute for talent: the best people remain successful, that is, those who know what they are looking for, and how to assess it before they actually do it. Those recruits who did not know what they were looking for and how to assess themselves, were termed as not successful. The result indicates that without knowing which emotional skills support success, training programmes cannot achieve optimal success.

4. In jobs of medium complexity (sales clerks and mechanics), a top performer is likely to be 12 times more productive than those at the bottom, and 85 per cent more productive than an average performer. In more complex jobs (insurance sales people and account managers), a top performer is likely to be 127 per cent more productive than the average. Competency research covering over 200 companies and organisations worldwide revealed that nearly one-third of this difference was due to technical skills and academic ability while two-thirds was due to emotional competence. In top leadership positions, over four-fifths of the difference was explained by emotional competence.

5. A national furniture retailer who hired sales persons on the basis of their emotional competence reported a higher rate of success among them. Among 515 senior executives analysed by the search firm, those who were primarily high on EQ were more likely to succeed than those who were stronger in either relevant previous experience or in IQ. In other words, EQ was a better predictor of success than either experience or high IQ. More specifically, executives high on EQ accounted for 74 per cent of the successes and only 24 per cent of the failures. The study examined executives from Latin America, Germany and Japan, and the findings were more or less similar across all three cultures.

6. After supervisors in a manufacturing plant received training in emotional competencies, such as how to listen more sympathetically and help employees resolve problems on their own, accidents decreased by 50 per cent, formal grievances decreased from an average of 15 per year to 3 per year, and the plant exceeded productivity goals by US $250,000. In another manufacturing plant, where supervisors received similar training, production increased by 17 per cent. There was no such improvement in productivity in a group of matched supervisors who were not trained in emotional competence.

7. In a large marketing organisation, sales agents selected on the basis of specific emotional competencies significantly outsold salespersons recruited in accordance with the company's old selection procedure. On an annual basis, sales agents selected on the basis of emotional competencies sold US $91,370 more than others, resulting in a net revenue increase of US $2,558,360. There was also 63 per cent lower turnover in terms of leaving the company during the first year, as compared to those selected by conventional methods.

8. Using standard methods to hire divisional presidents in a large beverage firm, 50 per cent left within two years, mostly because of poor performance. However, when selection was on the basis of emotional competencies such as initiative, self-confidence and leadership, only 6 per cent left in two years. Also, division leaders high on these competencies outperformed their targets by 15 to 20 per cent. Those who lacked these emotional competencies under-performed by almost 20 per cent.

9. In a national insurance company, sales agents who were weak in emotional competencies such as self-confidence, initiative and empathy, sold policies with an average premium of US $54,000, whereas those who were very strong in at least 5 of 8 key emotional competencies sold policies with premiums worth US $114,000.

10. The success of store managers in a retail chain was linked to their ability to handle stress. The most successful store managers were best able to deal with stress. Success was measured in terms of net profits, sales per square foot, sales per employee, and per dollar inventory investment.

11. Optimism is seen to be associated with increased productivity. New salespersons at Met Life who scored high in a test on 'optimism' sold 37 per cent more life insurance policies in the first two years than did pessimists.

12. A study of 130 executives showed that the way they handled their own emotions determined the extent to which people around them preferred to deal with them.

13. Sales representatives in a computer company who were hired on the basis of emotional competence were 90 per cent more likely to complete their training than those hired on the basis of other criteria.

On the basis of recent research, it may be concluded that EQ is a far more reliable indicator of success than IQ. It seems that what has been regarded as folk wisdom is now being corroborated by science. This is the greatest breakthrough in psychology in the 21st century, with profound implications for education, and for the organisation of society in general. Scientific work done in this area also confirms that it is possible to develop EQ. This may lead to improved interpersonal relations among human beings in the family, at the workplace and elsewhere.

Emotions developed through millions of years of evolutionary refinement help you to survive and thrive. If you do not listen to the messages sent by your emotions, you are not only unhappy, but also risk ill health and lower productivity. You will have to learn to communicate messages to others. For example, when your facial expression conveys anger or 'stay away', people usually do. On the other hand, when you smile, you communicate that it is safe to 'approach' you. Emotions are a critical survival tool for human beings. They provide the key to health, happiness and self-esteem. Emotions are the common bond that can potentially unite all human beings, and thus reduce conflict at the workplace. It is heartening to note that emotionally intelligent parents, teachers, managers and professionals can help raise the level of EQ in others.

Understanding your emotions, behaviours, feelings and thoughts will help you plan ways to change them. It should be remembered that EQ may be used to alleviate an unpleasant emotion. Fears can also be mitigated by modelling someone who is not as afraid as you are. You can develop other behaviours that counteract unwanted emotions. For example, activity overcomes depression, assertion counteracts anger, confronting fear counteracts fear, and relaxation counteracts hyperactivity of the workaholic.

Contrary to the popular belief that 'time heals', there is evidence to show that emotions such as fear, grief or the memory of a trauma, do not just fade away. They diminish in intensity if you repeatedly expose yourself to the unpleasant memories in a relaxed atmosphere or under less stressful conditions. If an unwanted emotion bothers you, it should be tackled first. Also, emotions have to be altered. It can be done, for example, by asking your friends to praise your healthy assertiveness and challenge your conformity. The skills listed here deal with basic raw emotions: anxiety, fear, anger and sadness. Of course, the same methods can be applied to the emotional aspects of any problem. Knowing that emotions are a crucial part of our lives, and are also fascinating, helps us to deal with them effectively.

SOME SIMPLE TIPS TO DEVELOP YOUR EQ

Any time you intend to learn new emotional skills, follow the golden rules given below:

- Contact someone who is good at handling emotions, or find a model
- Watch that person do it
- Notice signals
- Get the person to talk how he/she does it
- Practice doing it yourself with his or her guidance
- Ask the person to give you feedback
- Practice doing it on your own
- Seek feedback until you have mastered the skill
- Repeat steps

For detailed guidelines for training and development of EQ, refer to Chapter 6 of this book.

4

Emotional Skills that Managers should Learn

> What doesn't feel good to us normally doesn't feel good to others. But to understand the importance of this, we must first be in touch with our own feeling.

Emotional intelligence calls for the acquisition of certain emotional skills. Managers have to learn these skills to be star performers and achieve success in their professional life. What are these emotional skills? While identifying these skills, the definition of emotional intelligence as arrived at by the author in this book has been used. The three dimensions of emotional intelligence; emotional sensitivity, emotional maturity and emotional competency, represent these skills. Acquiring emotional competence may not mean having intellectual grasp over the concepts involved, although this may be one of the easiest approaches. Intellectual understanding is only a threshold process that is necessary for learning, but not sufficient for lasting improvement. Deeper changes require the retooling of ingrained habits of thought and emotion that managers will have to practice.

> The three dimensions of emotional intelligence—emotional sensitivity, emotional maturity and emotional competency—represent these skills.

Society is changing so rapidly that you can ill afford to remain the same for very long. You will need to understand the difference between being able to change easily and not wanting to change at all. How do you feel when you step out of your self-defined comfort zone? Can you master the art of handling these emotions so that you can push your comfort zone further and enjoy it? As a husband, wife, friend or even as a simple human being, you are often faced with other people's emotions. Being more skilled at handling your own emotions as well as those of others makes it less stressful for you to live in the world. You may perhaps realise, psychologically, the need to change your ways. Unless you can master the skills necessary for active emotional awareness, you continue to be tied to an intellectual path, losing touch with the deeper, stronger emotions that motivate the desire to act.

Our emotional intelligence is what determines our potential to learn practical skills. Our emotional competence shows how much of this potential is translated into on-the-job capabilities. For instance, being good at serving customers is an emotional competence based on empathy. Similarly, trustworthiness is a competence based on self-regulation. Both customer service and trustworthiness are competencies that can make people outstanding in their area of work. However, just being high in emotional intelligence does not necessarily guarantee that a person will have learned the emotional competencies that matter; it only means that he or she has excellent potential to learn these. For example, a person might be highly empathic, yet may not have learned the skills based on empathy that translate themselves into superior customer service, or the ability to coach or monitor staff, or the ability to bring together a diverse work team. The parallel in music would be, say, someone with a perfect pitch, and with the necessary training, becomes a maestro.

Emotional skills are clustered into groups, each based on a common, underlying emotional intelligence ability. These underlying abilities are vital if people are to successfully learn the competencies necessary to succeed at the workplace. If people are deficient in emotional skills, they will, for instance, be inept at persuading or inspiring others or leading teams or catalysing change. If their self-awareness is low, they will be oblivious to their own weaknesses and may lack the self-confidence that comes from the certainty of their strengths.

An inevitable fact is that emotional life is difficult to handle. Everyone experiences highs and lows. Balance is the key, and by using emotional intelligence you can escape moods that create problems. Can you activate yourself when you are down? Can you calm down when you are over activated? We all have emotions, but we can exercise some measure of control over how long these emotions last, and how we act on them. An emotionally intelligent manager will require these skills in varied measures. Some of the skills that can help in managing emotions in your personal life as well as in the workplace are listed below:

- Learn to Recognise your Emotions
- Learn to Empathise with Others
- Develop High Self-esteem
- Manage Emotional Upsets
- Be an Emotional 'Winner'
- Learn the Art of Influencing People
- Manage your Anger
- Other Related Areas

LEARN TO RECOGNISE YOUR EMOTIONS

Recognising and identifying emotions is a prerequisite for developing emotional intelligence. There is a major difference between experiencing emotions and recognising them. We all experience emotions but only a few among us can actually recognise them. Recognising your emotions is the ability to use the analytical capabilities of your brain. People who can identify and recognise their emotions have higher levels of emotional intelligence. Being clear about your emotions is necessary for living with a purpose. In the process, you will learn how to improve your EQ by controlling a particular emotion.

> If you are able to recognise your emotions you will also be able to manage them.

How do you recognise your emotions? A senior executive was heard saying, 'He does not know when he gets angry. It's only after he has released his pent-up feelings that he realises he was angry.'

On another occasion, a subordinate complained that he does not know how to identify and recognise the emotions of his boss. 'By the time I realise what he wants, it's all over,' he says. In order to accurately recognise your emotions, you need higher EQ competencies. Let us see what happens to the people who fail to recognise their emotions.

☞ The Derailed Executive

Let us diagnose a high profile career woman working in a nationalised bank. She always feels that nobody cares for her. She is smart, conscientious, well organised and industrious. She really cares about other people. But whenever there is a function and invitations are sent out, she invariably does not get invited. At office she hears of lunch plans in the making, but ends up eating alone at her table. There is a reason why she is not on anybody's guest list. She is an angry woman, but she does not know about it. Nor does she want to admit that she gets angry on trivial issues. Perhaps, she is angry because she did not get promoted, or her mother loved her sister more than her, or her boyfriend had cheated on her. There is no need to explore any more reasons. But whatever the reason(s), she does not want to acknowledge that she gets angry. Most of the time she concentrates on pushing away her emotions—something she is really good at. She convinces herself through constant mental chatter: 'No one ever gives me a chance...they're so unfair...it wasn't my fault.' She pushes these feelings out of her system but projects them on to everyone else. Since she is unable to recognise either her own emotions or those of others, she is often caught off guard and hurt by any direct confrontation. She is therefore always on her guard and defends herself at every turn. If, for example, the room feels warm, she will say that she was nowhere near the thermostat. When something upsets her, and most things do, it comes as a complete surprise to her, and her knee jerk response is 'I've done nothing wrong'. People sense the anger and try to avoid her. Rather than experience the pain of constant rejection, she is endlessly obsessed about how unfairly she is being treated and so perpetuates the cycle of emotional hurt.

Contd.

Contd.

> Have you been able to diagnose our high profile career woman? She changes her mood, rationalises and rehearses, and in doing so, changes the emotion she experiences from internal hurt to poorly concealed rage. If only she could learn to recognise all her emotions and not be caught off guard, she would definitely be able to develop the ability to manage her anger. And this would enable her to hear unpleasant things without becoming angry or bear hurt without expressing the hurt as hostility. She could become a much more desirable person to interact with and be noticed and welcome by all.

Many of us repeatedly take decisions without recognising an emotion, and which we regret later; we escape from realistic situations, raise our voice when not required, have doubts about ourselves and behave inappropriately at times. This happens when we are not able to recognise our emotions. Learn to recognise your emotion as it surfaces. Take over the emotion before it takes you over; don't wait till it becomes difficult for you to manage it. Never ignore your emotion, or you will become a victim of it. Also, notice physical symptoms like sweating, increased heartbeat and tenseness. React to an emotion only when you have adequate information with you about its likely consequences.

Study this cycle and observe how you tend to behave in a particular situation or with a particular person. This learning will help you to take decisions you will never regret. You will know how to choose the right responses. Practice this a few times, and you will see significant changes in your personality style. Why not to try right away?

LEARN TO EMPATHISE WITH OTHERS

Empathy is the ability to sense how other people feel. It is the key to success in your career, in friendships, in love and marriage and in child rearing. Being able to read non-verbal cues that contradict spoken

> 'Beginning today, treat everyone you meet as if they were going to be dead by midnight. Extend to them all the care, kindness and understanding you can muster. Your life will never be the same again.'

words, help you to know what is really going on in a situation. Some people can instantly empathise with others while others cannot. In the corporate world, small gestures like saying 'thank you', supporting employees' viewpoints, avoiding criticism of others or acknowledging employees' strengths, are the ingredients for fostering empathy among employees.

There are no great behavourial secrets to learn the emotional skill of empathising with others. If you are willing to accord top priority to supporting people, you will be blessed with results beyond your dreams. Managers often think of themselves as systems specialists, problem solvers or functional experts. They lose sight of the commonsense practicality that can motivate employees to do things willingly. The essence of good management is letting employees know what you expect, inspecting what is done, and supporting those things that are done well. If managers begin thinking in terms of doing things *for* people, instead of *to* them, they will experience a positive change in their working environment.

There are some actions you can take right away without increasing your budget, but which will fetch high returns. Make a list of all the people who work for you. Before the week is out, tell each one personally what he/she has contributed during the week and how much you appreciate his/her efforts. Avoid criticism at all costs (there is no such thing as constructive criticism, all criticisms are destructive). If you must correct someone, never do it after the event. If you can do this consistently, you would be justifying your salary as a professional manager. Organise informal meetings with your people. Listen and observe all that is happening. Instead of focusing on weaknesses, concentrate on strengths and things done well. Try to appreciate your employees' positive traits. As a manager, your words and actions will have a far greater impact than you expect. These techniques, you will find, have almost immediate effect. A concentrated, disciplined and sustained thrust in this direction will yield incredible returns.

To be empathetic you would need to be innovative. How innovative can you be? Do you realise the impact you have on others? Can you reduce or eliminate the negativities in your dealings with people? Are you willing to search and analyse so as to uncover positive contributions? Can you identify the strengths of all of your employees? Do you have something positive to say to everyone at the end of the task? Though this may seem simple and straightforward, it is a very difficult professional challenge. Just how good are you as a professional manager? If committed people produce results, how much love and money are you willing to invest to build that commitment and get those results? If you have not done any of these so far, go ahead and do something positive for someone.

Empathy is not just a romantic idea. Being able to understand another's feelings is not merely an abstract concept. If you are out of touch with your own feelings, you may not be able to understand empathy. You can empathise with others only when you are attuned to them. Attunement reflects how well you connect with, and react to, people. Successful people network well with others. When problems arise, people with empathy skills are better equipped to get the required advice and help from colleagues and are thus generally more successful in their projects. Those who need people, can read others and relate to their needs, are the lucky and successful ones. In the changing corporate and business world, the team, rather than the individual, is the basic work unit. When working in a team, you require a higher degree of empathy and related skills. Modern business recognises that the value of these skills is cost effective, and that it pays to have empathy in the organisation.

Your EQ tells you how you feel about others. For instance, your friend would love it if you would just remember his/her birthday and send your wishes; your boss would appreciate it if you would just take a little initiative and call a meeting when a problem arises, instead of waiting for someone else to point it out. Your subordinates would be happy if you would just say 'thank you' when they have accomplished the task assigned to them. In fact, the more empathetic you are about something, the greater the likelihood that people will act on your advice. Moreover, people tend to remember best those events that move them emotionally. Individuals who have distanced themselves from emotional intelligence, often have a hard time remembering what they had promised to do. Let us see the confession of an un-empathetic business manager.

> ### ☞ The Un-empathetic Business Manager
>
> When emotions start building up, emotional intelligence comes to the rescue. An un-empathetic manager confessed: I'm a hot head. I was extremely emotional. I'd take everything to heart and react strongly. It badly affected my relationships with people in the office: If they didn't see things my way, I'd get mad. It was my way or no way. I could not see things from their perspective; I would not compromise. That lack of emotional empathy worked against me. It prevented me from moving up; it got in the way of making decisions. If I was upset about something, I couldn't move on to the next project. It cost me money. I could not anticipate what people wanted from me. I was critical of others throughout. Whatever best they did it could never got registered in my mind. I was going to be a misfit. Then I attended a training session in emotional intelligence. It was a revelation. I had never encountered anything like this before. This was the missing piece in my life. I found that my empathy level was dangerously low. I saw how my emotions were controlling me and keeping me away from my people. I decided to upgrade my empathy skills. This has helped me immensely. Now if something is bothering me, I talk it over with my business partner, write it in my journal, talk to my field vice president right away. I let them know I'm upset; I don't let it fester. I'm more accepting now. Similarly, if I get a feeler that my employees wish to say something, I readily listen and make sincere efforts to mitigate their grievances. I realise you can have all kinds of emotions, but you don't have to let them run you. I now believe that emotional intelligence paves the way for improved interpersonal, intra-personal and professional relations.

DEVELOP HIGH SELF-ESTEEM

How you feel about yourself is the most tangible indication of self-esteem. Though high self-esteem primarily depends on your feelings about yourself, it is often bolstered by others also; people you share your feelings with. Feelings such as confidence, respect, being wanted and cared for, result in high self-esteem, which not only gives you real-

> Psychologists agree that the single most important trait of a healthy, happy, successful person is high self-esteem.

istic confidence in yourself but also in your ability to handle adversities in life. It leads to success at work and in personal relationships. It enables you to handle conflict, face challenges and perceive difficulties as learning opportunities. As a result, you are constantly growing and improving. On the other hand, low self-esteem leads to feelings of failure, and hence you are always either giving up or trying to prove yourself. There is a tendency to avoid confronting problems among persons with low EQ because they do not really believe that they can solve them. Consequently, other outlets, such as alcohol, work, exercise, academics, religion, self-righteousness, parenting, relationships or even drugs, are sought which provide a distraction and allow them to avoid facing difficult issues.

A sense of high self-esteem is one of the greatest gifts an organisation can give its employees, or parents can give their children. Yet most organisations are ill equipped to offer such a gift. They may offer high salaries, attractive perks, but not self-esteem. As a result, thousands of employees suffer from a wounded self-esteem inflicted by the most well-meaning of employers. Such employers can often undermine their employees' self-esteem in several ways including psychological invalidation, inappropriate expectations, harsh criticism, neglect, over-control, over-protectiveness and lack of emotional support and proper modelling. Well-intentioned employers may also cause damage by instilling fear, anxiety and dysfunctional belief systems in their employees. The feelings associated with or characteristics of high and low self-esteem are given below.

The table shows that self-esteem is a recognition of personal worth developed through a sense of competency, efficacy, connection to others and mutual respect. Self-esteem is also dependent on the ability to self-validate and act on perception or inner voice. Let us now see how self-esteem works in our lives.

Feeling of high self-esteem	Feeling of low self-esteem
Adequate	Alone
Admired	Attacked
Appreciated	Betrayed
Cared	Bitter
Competent	Coerced
Confident	Criticised
Controlled	Defeated
Cooperative	Defiant
Desired	Depressed
Important	Disrespected
Integrity	Distrustful
Joyful	Guilty
Loved	Helpless
Motivated	Inferior
Needed	Irritated
Optimistic	Isolated
Powerful	Jealous
Productive	Manipulated
Purposeful	Pessimistic
Respected	Powerless
Supported	Self-conscious
Sure	Tense
Trusted	Unappreciated
Understood	Uncomfortable
Useful	Unimportant
Valued	Unwanted
Wanted	Used
Worthy	Useless

☞ Who Sells More Insurance Policies

'I really can't believe that emotional intelligence makes such a great difference in the insurance sector,' says a retired General Manager who had served in the Life Insurance Company for 36 years and now

Contd.

Contd.

heads an internationally recognised training centre for young insurance salespersons in north India. 'Traditionally, insurance companies worldwide have believed that an academically brilliant sales person would sell more policies. But new research is proving them wrong. Any product, idea or service that you sell is really based on emotions and only later do you justify your choice with numbers and facts.

'What are the personality characteristics of an effective insurance salesperson? Whenever this question was posed to me, my reaction used to be that I have never ever looked into recruitment from this angle. I have by now "trained" hundreds of fresh insurance salespersons. We get trainees from all major insurance companies all over the world. We train them in general and financial aspects of insurance as they already stand selected by their parent companies. The parent companies induct people on the basis of written examination and the [salesperson's] academic background. Experience shows that half the recruits quit after the first year, and four out of five within 5 years. The reason is that selling life insurance means having the door slammed in your face repeatedly. You have to effectively handle frustration and take each refusal as a challenge rather than a setback. This is where the importance of self-esteem comes in. When optimists fail, they attribute the failure to something they can change, not to some innate weakness that they are unable to overcome. I do agree now that we do not need MBAs to sell insurance policies. The job can equally and effectively done by less academically brilliant persons. In the late nineties, I had to induct 25 new salespersons for my company. The best performance, to my surprise, was from a recruit who had a rural background, was seemingly unimpressive and to say the least, was not really academically bright. But he surpassed all expectations and sold policies worth Rs 4 million in the first three months, when his otherwise academically brilliant colleagues were still staggering at a target of around half a million. I discovered that successful recruits had a strong sense of optimism and self-esteem.

'I feel that the single most important virtue an insurance sales person must have is high self-esteem. In addition you require optimism, creativity, ability to collaborate and take initiatives to be successful in this profession. You have to, for example, imagine new

Contd.

Contd.

> ways to make your company's policies saleable. List all the details that are likely to compel customers to choose your company's policies over your competitors' and continuously analyse how you can improve upon these features. It is commonsense to use EQ in insurance business; unfortunately, this is not a common practice.
>
> 'Now, after an experience of more than three decades in this highly competitive field, I can say that if you are high on EQ, you are in tune with yourself and your potential. This will, in turn, help your organisation as well. In the insurance sector, if you know what risks to take, or avoid, you can do wonders. Your EQ helps you in other ways too. It can guide your decision-making ability to automatically process outcomes, questions and problems. It allows you to consider different alternatives and enables you to move faster. If customers feel you are genuinely listening to their problems, they will trust you and will reward you by giving you more and more business. Also, when your pitch to investors is based on EQ, you appear more reliable and passionate. Unfortunately, most of the insurance companies know about it but refuse to admit or change their recruitment practices.'

Manage Emotional Upsets

An emotionally upset person's performance at work will suffer; hence, being able to deal with both professional and personal upsets will help him or her achieve full productivity. It will also impact his or her perseverance, which is a vital skill in today's fast changing society. For instance, if you are a manager or a supervisor or providing customer service, you are often faced with other people's emotions. Being adept at handling your own emotion makes it less stressful for you to deal with other people. The ability to deal with emotional upsets is a powerful asset in building and/or maintaining your self-confidence. This enables you to believe in your own abilities and your own approach to tasks and problems. It also helps you to accept challenging tasks that other people tend to avoid. If you can deal with upsets easily and effortlessly, then you will become more comfortably aware of your feelings on a moment-to-moment basis.

We will discuss two kinds of situations that lead to emotional upsets: stress and conflict.

Stress is an important issue relating to emotional upsets. Today, stress is the major form of injury suffered by professionals and is a topic of interest to all. Stress is often described as the silent killer because the effects of stress are not readily apparent; they may either go undiagnosed or take a long time before they are manifested, leading to permanent damage. Stress can affect anyone. Psychologists have found that nowadays even a toddler of 5 years can suffer from stress.

The impact of stress on physical and psychological well-being is well documented. Is management, for instance, aware that members of the staff are angry, frustrated, anxious, lacking concentration or losing trust in the company? It could well be that they are either overworked or are subject to unwanted management pressure. Experience shows that employers who fail to treat workplace stress as an occupational

> Organisations which ignore stress tend to pay a heavy price.

health and safety issue may have to incur heavy costs. Employers who fail to view stress in its proper context also pay a heavy price through increased absenteeism, high staff turnover, decreased productivity, increased injuries and higher levels of litigation. Job-related stress can cause job-related dissatisfaction, which is in fact the simplest and most obvious psychological effect of stress. According to researchers, people who experience the highest level of stress have almost five times the risk of developing cardiovascular disease as compared to people with the lowest stress levels. Stress manifests itself in many psychological forms such as tension, anxiety, irritability, boredom and procrastination. Also, behaviour-related stress symptoms include changes in productivity, absenteeism and turnover, changes in eating habits, increased smoking or consumption of alcohol, rapid speech, fidgeting and sleep disorders. Do not be alarmed if you are told that stress has been instrumental in heart diseases, eating disorders, stroke, insomnia, ulcers, proneness to accident, cancer, decreased immunity, chronic headaches, diabetes, depression, substance abuse, chronic pain, irritable bowel syndrome and chronic fatigue. Many of these symptoms may be difficult to detect, but the appearance of any one of these symptoms should alert an employer that a problem might be developing. It would require an emotionally intelligent management to identify these negative emotions in time and take the desired corrective measures.

Stress is usually perceived in negative terms as caused by something bad (for example, the boss issuing a formal reprimand for poor performance). But there can also be a positive, pleasant side to stress caused by something good (for example, an employee being offered a job promotion in another location). Hence, stress may be considered as the interaction of an individual with the environment. Stress is therefore a dynamic condition in which an individual is confronted with an opportunity, a constraint, or a demand related to what he or she desires and for which the outcome is perceived to be both uncertain and unimportant. Stress is not always necessarily bad in itself.

As pointed out earlier, stress does not automatically have deleterious effects on individual employees or an organisation's performance. In fact, it is generally recognised that low levels of stress can even enhance job performance. For example, mild stress, such as getting a new supervisor or being involuntarily transferred, may intensify the desire for more information for the job. This may lead employees to new and better ways of doing their jobs. Also, mild levels of stress may lead to increased activity, change and overall improvement in performance. People in sales or creative fields (for example, newspaper journalists and television announcers who work under time pressure) may actually benefit from mild levels of stress. Consider the superior performance that an athlete or a stage performer gives in 'clutch' situations. Such individuals often use stress positively to rise to the occasion and perform at or near their peak. On the other hand, professionals like police officers and physicians may not benefit from constant mild stress.

Interestingly, stress does not have the same impact on everyone. There are individual differences in coping with stressful situations. Some people go to pieces at the slightest provocation, while others seem unflappable even in extremely stressful conditions. It is here that EQ comes to our rescue and guides us to respond appropriately to different stressors.

There are three potential sources of stress: environmental, organisational and individual. Whether they lead to actual stress depends on individual differences related to job experience and personality. When you experience stress, it may be manifested as psychological, physiological or behaviourial symptoms. For example, a group that faces frequent work-related dangers is law enforcement officers. Stress is the hidden assailant in law enforcement. Job stress among police officers often leads to alcohol abuse, disruption of normal sleeping and eating patterns, poor nutrition, paranoia, anger and fear. It has also been observed that stress is most frequently caused by factors like marital and other family difficulties, difficult relationships with fellow officers, management-related problems, trauma associated with death, issues related to retirement, financial problems, debt management, alcoholism and drug abuse. Organisational stress is the outcome of multidimensional factors. Besides potential stressors that occur outside the organisation, there are stressors associated with the organisation itself. Although the organisation is made up of groups and individuals, there are other macro-level dimensions, unique to the organisation, that may contain potential stressors such as policies, unfair and arbitrary performance reviews, pay inequalities, inflexible rules, rotating working shifts, ambiguous procedures, frequent relocation, unrealistic job descriptions, centralisation, lack of participation in decision-making, line-staff conflicts, lack of privacy, excess noise, heat or cold and poor/inadequate feedback about performance. It has been noted that as organisations become larger and more complex, there are an increasing number of accompanying stressors for individual employees. As companies of today and tomorrow compete in an increasingly competitive global marketplace, organisational stressors can become even more severe. In a recent survey of CEOs of Fortune 500 companies, over three-fourths of the respondents agreed with the statement that large companies would have to push their managers harder if they are to compete successfully with other global competitors.

Some people thrive on stressful situations, while others are overwhelmed by them. What accounts for the varying ability of people to handle stress? Needless to say, it is your emotional response to a particular situation that makes the difference. EQ helps you to cope with stressful situations. Stress management, therefore, largely depends upon striking an emotional balance between a potential stress condition and your reaction to it. In addition, there is increasing evidence that social support and interpersonal relationships with co-workers or supervisors can buffer the impact of stress. The underlying logic is that social support acts to mitigate the negative effects of stress. Only professionals with a higher degree of EQ can develop such an effective support system.

Conflict is another emotional upset you face in day-to-day life. Conflict consists of interactive, opposing behaviours between two or more persons, groups or larger social systems with incompatible goals. A survey of managers by the American Management Association revealed that managers spent about 24 per cent of their time dealing with conflicts. Considering the amount of time spent on handling conflict, it seemed reasonable to expect conflict resolution to be an important factor determining managerial performance.

Conflict resolution also requires understanding and application of emotional intelligence. Conflict refers to all types of opposition or antagonistic interaction. There is constructive as well as destructive conflict. Constructive conflict can lead individuals and organisations to become more creative and productive by rising to the challenge. Destructive conflict consumes personal and organisational resources in hostility and bitterness. Undesirable conflict virtually always escalates into a serious problem if left unresolved. Once a conflict is diagnosed, a resolution technique must be chosen. There are situations where conflict avoidance makes sense. Frequently, however, avoiding issues simply aggravates the problem. The way a conflict is resolved by managers is significant both in terms of effective individual and organisational performance, and in terms of human satisfaction and health at the workplace. Individual conflicts and their expression have been studied by psychologists who argue that an interactive approach must be adopted in dealing with individual conflict, one that takes into account the persons involved in a conflict situation and how and why the discontent is expressed.

An extensive range of choices is available to individuals to express their disagreement with one another in case of a conflict. These include both conventional actions (going slow or quitting a job) and unconventional actions (rule breaking or pilfering). Managers should be trained to understand how, by adopting effective two-way communication and appropriate managerial techniques, the occurrence of conflicts can be realistically reduced. The task of motivating subordinates on how to handle conflicts effectively is not an easy one. Over time, this has not only become more complex, but increasingly more important. Managers must resolve conflicts effectively in order to successfully achieve both organisational as well as individual goals. If a manager is able to recognise his or her own strengths and weaknesses, clearly understand the requirements of the job, use his or her strengths and overcome weaknesses through continuous learning on the job, only then will he or she be effective in conflict resolution. This can be achieved through an understanding of EQ, as was seen in a commercial bank (see box below).

☞ Managing Emotional Upsets in a Commercial Bank

Introduction
A private sector commercial bank opened its new branch in a high-end business market of New Delhi. Despite the trained staff and good infrastructure, it did not attract new customers in the first six months of its commencing operations. The bank manager was at sea to decipher where and what had gone wrong. There was pressure from the top management to either perform or quit. He tried all management tricks to break through the employees' habits and translate them into new behaviour at work, but nothing worked. 'These employees just do not want any positive change,' he lamented.

Contd.

Contd.

Diagnosis
In the middle of the financial year, the manager happened to read an article on EQ in a national daily and decided it was worth looking into. He invited the EQ experts to conduct experiments and suggest interventions. The EQ team scheduled a one-day workshop with all employees, on a weekend, for initiation and self-assessment. They were asked to make EQ a personal commitment and gradually make it a part of their daily work. An EQ test was conducted and its scores tabulated. Sharp differences were noticed among the managers at inter-personal level. Most of them failed to qualify in most of the major parameters of emotional competence, especially in their ability to handle emotional upsets. The single most frequently mentioned factor descriptive of their behaviour was that their stress levels were unreasonably high which made them too harshly critical, insensitive or demanding. The group reacted to stress and conflict in a defensive manner by denying, covering up or even passing on the blame. The other specific emotional competencies found lacking were self-control, job-related dissatisfaction, tension, anxiety, irritability, boredom, rigidity and poor relationships. Those who failed to deliver, typically, were overly ambitious and only too ready to get ahead at the expense of other people. Due to the insensitive characteristic of the group, they were unable to build a strong network of cooperative, mutually beneficial relationships. Neither were they able to adapt to changes in organisational culture, nor accept or respond to feedback. They could neither listen nor learn.

Intervention
The EQ team facilitated the feedback of each member of the bank's staff from their respective superiors, peers and subordinates. The data collected was on certain critical emotional competencies that were found lacking. The feedback received in the 'focus group' as well as 'individual interactions' was then communicated to the concerned employee, followed up by psychological coaching. They were asked to first interpret their own scores and see what changes could be made to improve their individual performance as well as that of the bank. They were coached to recognise and name the underlying emotions in each related feedback. This process helped

Contd.

Contd.

the employees know how they are looked upon by their peers, and to what extent their own views match others' perceptions. In addition to the feedback and coaching, the group was also trained in specific emotional skills as thrown up by the diagnosis process. The EQ experts then developed short-term as well as long-term vision for the bank, based on existing and proposed-to-be-acquired emotional skills. Two short-term seminars on emotional intelligence were conducted with the aim of improving the employees' EQ skills.

Outcome

Those who received EQ intervention reported that they could now handle pressure and control angry outbursts from customers effectively. Most of them admitted that they were able to bear stress, remain calm, confident and dependable in the heat of crises. They had now learned to assume responsibility by admitting their mistakes and failures, taking appropriate action to fix problems, and moving on without lamenting about their lapses. They were more appreciative of diversity and were able to get along with all types of people. Employees and management could see changes in the day-to-day operations. There was improvement in communication, respect had increased as people sought to understand one another rather than be judgemental or take others/things for granted. They were now more willing to accept advice and feedback. These 'soft' changes resulted in an improved bottom line.

Variable	2003	2004
Customer Satisfaction (on a 10-point scale)	2.1	8.4
Market share of the area	26%	80%
Revenue Increase	50%	90%
Absenteeism	8%	<2%
Employee Grievances	22%	<3%
Stress Management	Dormant	Active
Conflict Resolution	Dormant	Active

After the EQ intervention, one client commented, 'everything looks so beautifully different here. The people around here are no longer the same. They behave differently now.' The manager

Contd.

> declared in a meeting at the end of the financial year, 'the unexpected turnaround has finally happened. The results and relationships are the witnesses to the same. I never knew that an emotionally empowered individual or organisation could bring in so much of happiness and profits in such a short time.' The employees acknowledged that the EQ training had helped them address issues that were keeping them from optimal performance. A lady employee smiled, 'It has transformed my personal life too. I understand my family better now and they also appreciate my viewpoint.'

BE AN EMOTIONAL 'WINNER'

To be emotionally intelligent means to be an emotional winner and not an emotional loser. When a person recognises another with a smile, a nod, a frown or a verbal greeting, he or she is using one or the other emotional network. These networks elicit a variety of emotions, ranging from anger, anxiety, frustration, sorrow, contentment or disappointment to affection, peace, trust, appreciation and motivation. This is where emotional intelligence comes into play: it tells a person how to react to the various different emotions of life. An emotionally intelligent person is in a better position to understand his or her own emotions and those of others, and so can take the correct decision in any situation. This may be explained through notions such as 'winners' and 'losers'. Each human being is born as someone new, someone who has never existed before. Each one is born with the capacity to win in life. Each person has a unique way of seeing, hearing, touching, tasting and thinking. Each one has his or her unique potentialities and limitations. Each can be a significant, thinking, aware and creative being: a productive person, a winner. The words winner and loser can have many meanings. When we refer to a person as a winner, we do not

> Few people are 100 per cent winners or losers. It is a matter of degree.
> The art of influencing situations can make you either a star performer or a disastrous failure.

necessarily mean that it is someone who makes another lose. A winner, to us, is one who responds authentically by being credible, trustworthy, responsive and genuine, both as an individual and as a member of society. A loser, on the other hand, is someone who fails to respond authentically. Few people are 100 per cent winners or losers; it is a matter of degree. Winners or losers respond to situations they encounter, differently.

A 'winner' knows that there is:	A 'loser' is someone who always laments:
• A time to be aggressive and a time to be passive	'If only I had married someone else...'
• A time to be together and a time to be alone	'If only I had a different job...'
• A time to fight and a time to love	'If only I had finished school...'
• A time to work and a time to play	'If only I had been handsome/beautiful...'
• A time to cry and a time to laugh	'If only my spouse had stopped drinking...'
• A time to confront and a time to withdraw	'If only I had been born rich...'
• A time to speak and a time to be silent	'If only I had better parents...'
• A time to hurry and a time to wait	'If only I had genuine friends...'

The winners are fully attentive and completely involved in their work and perform at their peak because they reflect high EQ. Others perceive them as accessible and engaged, and see how they contribute their creative ideas, energy and intuitions. The others, the losers, are all too familiar—they go through their work as a routine, obviously bored, or otherwise disconnected. In a sense, they may as well not have shown up. An example is a receptionist at a hotel who hated her job. She says, 'Sitting up here in front and smiling and typing and being friendly, it's useless. It's just a role, and there isn't any satisfaction in it for me. These eight or nine hours is a waste.'

In contrast, another receptionist in the same hotel considered the same job as refreshing, rewarding and full of opportunities. She says, 'you interact with new faces every other minute. It's quite interesting. I do not get bored for even a second during the entire day's work.' Let us see the following case to prove this point further.

☞ Winner versus Loser

Winners and losers react to identical situations differently. There is this case of two executives who were refused a promotion because of negative evaluations by their superior. One reacted to the setback with rage and fantasised about killing his boss; he complained to anyone who would listen and went on a drinking binge. 'It seemed like my life was over,' he said later. He avoided his boss, lowering his head when they passed each other in the hall. 'Even though I was angry and felt cheated,' he added,' deep down I feared that the boss was right, that I am worthless, that I had failed, and there was nothing I could do to change that.'

In contrast, the other executive, although equally stunned and angry, had a more open mind: 'I can't say I was surprised, really. He and I have such different ideas, and we've argued a lot.' The executive went home and talked this matter over with his wife to figure out what had gone wrong and what he could do about it. Engaging in such introspection, he realised that he had not been giving his maximum effort. With that knowledge, his anger faded, and he resolved to talk to his boss. The result: 'I had some discussions with him and things went very well. I guess he was troubled about what he had done, and I was troubled about not working up to my potential. Since then, things have been better for both of us.'

You may have guessed that the key competence that mattered here was EQ, which hinges on how we interpret our setbacks. A loser, like the first executive, saw the setback as conforming to some fatal flaw in him that could not be changed. The net result of such a defeatist attitude was, of course, a feeling of pessimism and helplessness: If you're doomed to fail, why try? The other executive, a winner, in contrast, sees a setback as a result of factors he has the power to do something about, not some flaw or deficiency in himself. Like the second executive, a winner can deal with a setback by finding a positive response.

Being a winner requires not being overwhelmed by anxiety, but being open to others. It needs perseverance. This means total attention to and immersion in the task on hand. As a winner, you are more attuned to those around you and to the needs of the situation, and you adapt fluidly to what is needed. In other words, you are 'in flow'. And that can help you to be a winner in most situations.

LEARN THE ART OF INFLUENCING PEOPLE

Your ability to impact and influence others is closely related to your ability to connect and use your emotions. You will agree that people are rarely influenced by logic alone; emotions are equally important. When you work with others, with your emotions, you can influence the behaviour of others and the work can become enjoyable and productive. Being at ease with emotions also makes it easier to relate to different types of people. The art of effectively influencing people at the workplace varies from person to person. For example, people with varying levels of EQ have varying degrees of influence on others. In the following example, let us see how this emotional skill is used by people.

> ### ☞ The Merger of Two Firms
>
> After the merger of two of the largest financial firms in the US, the press heralded the event as a crowning achievement. Within weeks of the announcement, numerous meetings were held in the two firms, detailing just how the two heavyweight companies would merge into a single giant. As is usual in the case of such mergers, hundreds of employees were expected to lose their jobs since many functions would be duplicated between the two firms. But how could this news be conveyed to the employees without making the reality worrisome?
>
> One department head in the firm conveyed the information in the worst possible manner. He gave a gloomy, even menacing, speech: 'I don't know what I'm going to do, but don't expect me to be nice to you. I have to fire half the people here, and I'm not exactly
>
> *Contd.*

Contd.

> sure how I'm going to make that decision, so I'd like each of you to tell me your background and qualifications so that I can start firing you.' His counterpart in the other firm did better. His message was upbeat. 'We think this new company will be a very exciting platform for our work, and we're blessed with talented people from both organisations to work with. We'll make our decisions as quickly as we can, but not until we're positively sure we've collected enough information, to be fair. We'll update you every few days on how we're doing. And we'll decide both on the basis of objective performance data plus qualitative abilities, like teamwork.'
>
> You may have noticed that the art of influencing the people by the two department heads varied. In the former firm, everyone was demotivated. They were heard saying, 'I'm not being treated fairly.' They were bitter, demoralised and said, 'I don't know if I even want to work for this firm anymore.' In the second organisation, the employees were more motivated because they were excited about the prospects. They knew even if they did not end up with a job, it would be a fair decision.

The art of influencing people entails handling their emotions. Both department heads were influential, but in completely opposite ways.

Star performers are skilled at sending emotional signals that make them powerful communicators, and enable them to sway an audience, that is, make them leaders. Apart from this, they have high EQ. On the other hand, those who fail to understand the emotions of others, bring poor management results to an organisation, and are generally low on EQ.

Manage Your Anger

Everyone gets angry at some point of time or other. This is natural and easy. But the management of anger is not easy. It requires learning of specific skills to handle anger. Let us see how anger influences our personality and whether it can or cannot be managed. That anger kills, shortens the life span, greatly increases the risk of many life-threatening diseases including heart disease, stroke, cancer and high blood pressure, and the incidence of depression, anxiety and other emotional disorders, is well known. Alcoholism, drug ad-

> Anger management is like using traffic lights. The red light means stop, calm down; the amber light means think through the problem; and the green light means a positive, non-aggressive solution.

diction, and other compulsive behaviours such as workaholism are strongly associated with anger. Even extramarital relations can be adduced to uncontrolled anger. Angry people complain more of aches and pains than others, and are prone to colds, headaches and upset stomachs. Laboratory experiments have shown that even subtle forms of anger impair problem-solving abilities and general performance. Anger leads to a narrow and rigid mental focus, obscuring the possibility of any alternative perspective. At the workplace, anger has an adverse impact on performance. It makes you a 'reactoholic', that is, reacting to other people's 'push buttons'; it makes you a powerless reactor rather than a powerful actor.

There is no attempt to define anger as a negative or positive emotion. Practical experience shows that often in personal and work situations 'anger' is known to be a positive emotion, if used consciously. Using anger sometimes gets a job done quickly and effectively. Anger is based on your not being conscious of your own, true feelings and is always a reaction to deeper feelings of hurt and vulnerability. Anger destroys positive feelings through an urge to avenge or punish which can quickly degenerate into self-righteousness. It creates power struggles; its only purpose is to exert power over someone else or prevent another from exerting power over you.

An angry person tends to have only one 'right way' of doing things which, if selected in anger, is seldom the best. Yet, conventional wisdom says there is nothing you can do when angry which you cannot do better when not angry. Psychologists insist that anger can be managed through emotionally intelligent reaction. You need to learn some emotional skills.

Do not allow anger to keep you from the success you can otherwise achieve. Learn how to manage anger before anger regulates you. In the world today there is a great deal of anger, some of which can be dangerous. People become enraged at the prospect of feeling disregarded, unimportant, accused, guilty, distrusted, devalued, rejected, powerless and unloved. These emotional turbulences are often attributed to family members, co-workers, and even society at large, thus making individuals powerless to exercise regulation. Emotional management of anger is possible only through compassion for oneself, restoring core values and thus making it possible to have compassion for others. Anger management uses the principles of emotional intelligence: being aware of an internal experience, being able to control the meaning of your emotional experience and cultivating empathy for the emotional experience of others.

> There is no such thing as uncontrollable anger.

Simultaneously, apply emergency tactics. In order to avoid bad feelings and avoid hurting yourself and those you love, learn to know that you do have the absolute power to stop hurting people you love even though you feel hurt and angry. You have a lot more inner strength than you realise and you do not need to lash out in response to anger. You should learn to detect the early signs of anger; what, for instance, does aggression feel like in your head, eyes, mouth, neck, shoulders, chest, back and hands. Anger arises from hurt. Focus on the hurt, not the anger. What is it that hurt you, hurt him or her? How can you improve the situation? Once you ask yourself these questions, you need not be abusive. Know that when you are angry, you are not yourself. The angry you is not the real you. Anger is merely a symptom of hurt. Finally, remember that the simplest solution is to take time out (leave the room or the house) if you cannot find another solution. The effects of anger have more to do with its duration than its frequency and intensity. Do you know how to judge the duration of anger? The normal experience of overt anger lasts only a few minutes. Subtle forms of anger, such as resentment, impatience, irritability and grouchiness, can persist for hours and even days at a time.

Emotional management of anger not only increases emotional intelligence, but also eliminates problems of resentment, divorce, domestic violence, child abuse, alcohol/drug relapse, emotional abuse, teen violence, shame, resentment, feelings of powerlessness and low self-esteem. It improves the emotional quality of your life, job performance, social skills and family relationships by increasing your compassion, interest, enjoyment, intimacy and commitment. Anger is a reaction to psychological hurt or threat of hurt in the form of a diminished sense of self. Vulnerability to psychological hurt depends entirely on how you feel about yourself. When your sense of self is weak or disorganised, even the most trivial thing can make you irritable or angry. When it is solid and well integrated, insults and frustrations in life just roll off your back. For instance, if you have had a bad day, if you are feeling guilty or have experienced a failure, or feeling disregarded, devalued, or irritable, you may come home to find your child's shoes in the middle of the floor and may burst out, 'That lazy, selfish, inconsiderate, little child.' However, when you come home after a great day of feeling fine about yourself and see the same shoes in the middle of the floor, you think, 'Oh, that's just funny,' and not think twice about it. This is true to all other real time life situation where you can decide to react positively, if you get angry.

Needless to say, anger management is an emotional competency that is essential for the survival and good health of any organisation and its productivity. The art of anger management also helps individual managers to understand, visualise and take corrective measures as and when required. Employees and employers can both benefit if they learn the art of handling anger in a way that is emotionally intelligent. In the current industrial environment where strikes, violence, union rivalry, and so on, have become a regular feature, an emotional response is the key to handling difficult situations. The following case study will help to understand this better.

Learn emotional skills to handle unwanted emotions. What to do when you are feel angry, passive, frustrated, jealous or cheated? Honestly, you need to have some skills or competencies to handle difficult emotional problems affecting your life and health. One of the greatest competencies is to delay the gratification of satisfying a particular dominant emotion on the spur of the moment.

☞ The Angry Woman

Here is the case of a qualified professional. She is the CEO of a top business house that she inherited from her family. She is good in the technical aspects of her job, but does not adapts herself emotionally and loses temper very easily. Despite her professional expertise she has a totally disorganised personality and no sense of rationality when she acts. Her temper is more painful to bear and she often gets angry with her subordinates who usually prefer to remain silent. Being impatient, she orders that every job be completed 'yesterday'. She feels that what she does is perfect and that what she says is the gospel truth. She is highly suspicious and attributes this trait to her family. Being unable to trust anyone, she feels depressed in interpersonal relations. She lacks empathy and expresses anger to satisfy her own psychological needs. She vents her anger on her surroundings for no valid reason and has a thousand excuses to justify such behaviour. She thus distracts herself from experiencing unpleasant feelings by blaming others. While attending to her job, she inadvertently says something that offends people in the organisation. Sometimes when people raise the issue, she simply asks how people could possibly get offended about such trivial things. Her personality reflects her turbulent upbringing and her tragic experiences and frustrations at all levels.

She is an angry woman, not emotionally intelligent. She is smart, but has a negative attitude. She cannot handle many complex problems relating to anger at the workplace and elsewhere. Unfortunately, she does not have a positive attitude and in the process harms herself as well as the people around her. She tends to be a misfit in the organisation and rationalises her behaviour by criticising others. People with low EQ do have emotions, and these feelings can reach such an intensity that they can erupt. Indeed, such people are more likely to become emotionally overwhelmed than those who consistently recognise the physical signals of emotion, because suppressed emotions can eventually rise to the surface, causing physical ailments and unexpected emotional outbursts.

In simple words, have patience and buy yourself some time before jumping to take any action. During angry situations, for example, listen to the other's point of view, even if it takes a while. This will greatly decrease your chances of overreacting to a situation and will give others time to figure out the genesis of the problem and result in cooling down the situation. EQ experts say that even if you count 10 with closed eyes the anger fades away as it usually does not last for more than 6 to 10 seconds. Being flexible in approach solves many seemingly unsolvable problems.

OTHER RELATED AREAS

And finally, development of EQ forcefully impacts your life in many ways. EQ requires the development of certain specific emotional skills. Some of the management areas where emotional skills can be developed to have gainful outcome are:

Corporate culture: Creating an environment where employees feel safe, trusted, special, needed, included, important, cooperative, focused, productive, motivated, respected and valued.

Hiring: Selecting employees who relatively high on emotional intelligence, that is, emotionally sensitive, aware, optimistic, resilient, positive and responsible.

Customer service: Develop EQ to help your customers feel heard, understood, helped, served, respected, valued and important.

High technology management: Helping technical experts in improving their emotional and people skills, that is, creating a high-tech, high-touch workplace.

Turnover: Realising turnover reduction by helping employees feel appreciated, recognised, supported, challenged, rewarded and respected.

Training: Raising EQ at all levels of the business through emotional literacy and EQ awareness workshops.

Productivity: Enhancing intrinsic motivation, increasing employee commitment, cooperation and cohesion. Reducing time spent on conflicts, turf-battles, defensiveness and insecurity.

Goal setting: Setting goals based on feelings. For example, setting customer satisfaction as a goal and setting similar goals for employees, seeking feedback on feelings and measuring and tracking performance.

Emotional support: Mitigating negative emotions such as fear, worry, anxiety and stress. These negative emotions lower the functioning of the immune system, increase blood pressure, increase the risk of heart attacks and cancer, prolong recovery times and cause migraine headaches. On the other hand, it has been seen that providing emotional support leads to tangible health benefits.

Leadership: A leader with high EQ is emotionally aware. Such a leader is also able to read universalised emotions in others, is emotionally literate in the sense that he or she is able to concisely articulate emotions; and has a broad vocabulary of feeling words. Thus, such a leader does not easily become defensive or angered. Apart from acknowledging fears and encouraging others to do likewise, the leader is empathic and accepts others and shows compassion, instead of being demanding and intolerant. Not only does the leader treat all feelings with respect, but is also inspiring and motivating.

5

Emotional Intelligence: The Empirical Evidence

If you look at the historical roots of emotional intelligence, you will find that when psychologists began research on intelligence, they focused on non-emotional aspects such as thinking, cognition, intellect, memory and problem-solving (read IQ). However, there were researchers who recognised early on that emotional aspects such as feelings, moods and non-cognition were equally important (read EQ). We will present, in this chapter, a review of all significant research work done in the field of emotional intelligence.

I   Defining Emotional Intelligence
II Levels of EQ Required for Various Jobs
III Emotional Intelligence Competencies
IV EQ in the Indian Perspective
V   Do Different Professions Require Different Levels of EQ?
VI Emotional Intelligence of IAS Officers
VII Emotional Intelligence and Leadership Behaviour
VIII Relation between EQ and IQ among Adolescents
IX EQ and Managerial Effectiveness: An International Study
X   EQ and Well-being of Adolescents
XI The Soft Art of being a Tough Leader
XII Emotional Intelligence and Stress Management
XIII Managing Human Capital: An EQ Perspective
XIV The Making of an EQ Test
XV Other Research Studies

This chapter contains scientific data and research. The general reader may wish to skip it.

I. Defining Emotional Intelligence

E.L. Thorndike (1920) had long ago identified a dimension of intelligence and named it *social intelligence*, and described it as the 'ability to understand and manage men and women, boys and girls to act wisely in human relations. It is an ability that shows itself abundantly in the nursery, on the playground, in factories, and sales rooms'. However, he found that measuring these traits was as not as simple as measuring IQ. He realised that social intelligence was a complex amalgam of several abilities, or of an enormous number of specific social habits and attitudes. His references to social intelligence included three elements: (*a*) the individual's attitudes towards society such as politics, economics, science and values such as honesty; (*b*) social knowledge such as being well versed in contemporary issues and general knowledge about society; and (*c*) the individual's capacity for social adjustment, such as interpersonal relations and family bonding. It may be noticed that the third aspect of Thorndike's definition of social intelligence did contain elements like 'ability to deal with people' and 'introversion and extroversion' types of personality, which is more akin to today's emotional intelligence. However, it may be clarified that Thorndike's definition included almost everything relating to human intelligence ranging from social, psychological, economic, emotional, personality types, affective and non-affective. As far as the present discussion is concerned, we may infer that Thorndike did refer to emotional aspects of intelligence in his definition of social intelligence as early as in 1920. His contentions are of great scientific help to modern researchers trying to establish the construct validity of emotional intelligence.

> EQ is the ability to understand and manage men and women, boys and girls to act wisely in human relations.

D. Wechsler (1940) defined intelligence as 'the aggregate or global capacity of the individual to act purposefully, to think rationally, and to deal effectively with his environment'. As early as 1940, he referred to 'intellective' as well as 'non-intellective' elements, by which he meant affective, self, and social factors. Furthermore, Wechsler proposed that the non-intellective abilities, that is, emotional abilities, are essential to determine one's ability to succeed in life. He found emotional intelligence to be an integrated with an individual's personality development. However, his views on emotional abilities did not attract much attention and psychologists the world over continued to define intelligence in terms of an individual's intellective or thinking ability. In fact, a great part of the world, especially the developing and under-developed countries, still believes that it is your 'academic achievements' that matter for success in life.

> Emotional abilities are essential to determine one's ability to succeed in life.

Howard Gardner (1993) writes about 'multiple intelligence' and proposed that 'intra-personal' and 'interpersonal' intelligences are as important as the type of intelligence typically measured by IQ and other related tests. He says that 'my intelligence does not stop at my skin' and it constitutes tools such as his computer and its database, his professional colleagues and others whom he can correspond with through e-mails. Gardner ascribed interpersonal intelligence to people who are leaders among their peers and are good at communicating. Also, they seem to understand others' feelings and motivations. He further elaborated that interpersonal intelligence does exist, and people with this kind of intelligence may be shy but are aware of their own feelings and self-motivated too. Unfortunately, psychologists largely ignored Gardner's references to 'emotional intelligence' and his definition of 'intelligence' was widely accepted as being dominated by 'rational intelligence'. Even today, Gardner's modern research is a reflection of his passion with the concept that he defines as linguistic, logical–mathematical, bodily–kinesthetic, spatial intelligence, musical intelligence, interpersonal intelligence and intra-personal intelligence. His reference to 'interpersonal and intra-personal

> Interpersonal intelligence relates to people who are leaders among their peers and are good at communicating.

intelligence' and its interpretation has, so far, attracted little from the academic world. Nonetheless, the fact remains that Gardner did mention emotional intelligence as a concept to define 'inter-personal' and 'intra-personal' intelligence.

Peter Salovey and John Mayer (1990) coined the term 'emotional intelligence' and described it as 'a form of social intelligence that involves the ability to monitor one's own and others' feelings and emotions, to discriminate among them, and to use this information to guide one's thinking and action'. For instance, they found in one study that when a group of people saw an upsetting film, those who scored high on emotional clarity (which is the ability to identify and give a name to a mood that is being experienced) recovered more quickly. In another study, individuals who scored higher in the ability to perceive accurately, understand, and appraise others' emotions were better able to respond flexibly to changes in their social environments and build supportive social networks. Salovey and Mayer (1997) further elaborated that emotional intelligence was 'the ability to perceive emotions, to access and generate emotions so as to assist thought, to understand emotions and emotional knowledge, and to reflectively regulate emotions so as to promote emotional and intellectual growth'. Emotional intelligence, according to them, involves areas such as (*a*) *identifying emotions*: the ability to recognise how you and those around you are feeling; (*b*) *using emotions*: the ability to generate emotion, and then reason with this emotion; (*c*) *understanding emotions*: the ability to understand complex emotions and emotional 'chains', how emotions transition from one stage to another; and (*d*) *managing emotions*: the ability which allows you to manage emotions in yourself and in others'.

> Salovey and Mayer coined the term 'emotional intelligence'.

Peter Salovey is Chairman of the Department of Psychology at Yale University and conducts research in areas such as psychological significance and function of human moods and emotions.

Daniel Goleman (1998) defines emotional intelligence as 'the capacity for recognising our own feelings and those of others, for motivating ourselves, and for managing emotions well in ourselves and in our relationships. Emotional intelligence describes abilities distinct from, but complementary to, academic intelligence or the purely cognitive capacities measured by IQ'. He has also identified a set of emotional competencies that differentiate individuals from one other. The competencies fall into four clusters: (*a*) *self-awareness*: the capacity for understanding one's emotions, one's strengths and one's weaknesses; (*b*) *self-management*: the capacity for effectively managing one's motives and regulating one's behaviour; (*c*) *social awareness*: the capacity for understanding what others are saying and feeling, and why they feel and act as they do; and (*d*) *social skills*: the capacity for acting in such a way that one is able to obtain the desired results from others and reach personal goals. Goleman explains that these competencies assist leaders to inspire organisations to greatness, salespeople to build strong and profitable customer relationships, and employees to delight customers they deal with every day. Moreover, these competencies can and should be taught to children in the early stages of life. It can be seen that Goleman has borrowed extensively from earlier exponents of general intelligence in the field of psychology, in his definition of emotional intelligence. Moreover, his contentions are largely based on his 'personal experiences' as a reporter, for many years, on brain and behavioural science with *The New York Times*. Additionally, Goleman prefers to call his model of emotional intelligence as 'theory of performance' rather than 'theory of personality'. His emphasis is on making a business case for emotional intelligence that builds on paradigms of emotional competencies. He has, however, not succeeded in telling the scientific world the distinction between the 'emotional competencies' and 'emotional personality traits' of an individual. A perusal of his recent writings reveal that he talks more about the 'theories of personality' propounded by psychologists such as Thorndike, Gardner and others. His independence from the personality theory has not been substantiated by the theory of performance. The basis on which he advocates widely published guidelines to take

> Emotional intelligence describes abilities distinct from, but complementary to, academic intelligence measured by IQ.

the concept of emotional intelligence away from the theory of personality and towards the theory of performance, may not be acceptable to modern-day psychologists.

Dr Goleman is founder and Chairman of the Consortium for Research on Emotional Intelligence in Organisations, based in the Graduate School of Applied and Professional Psychology at Rutgers University. The Consortium seeks to recommend best practices for developing emotional competence. He is yet to arrive at a widely acceptable definition of emotional intelligence and has, in fact, revised his own definition several times in the recent past. He has urged researchers worldwide to carry out 'original research' to establish the 'construct validity' of the definition of emotional intelligence. However, to his credit, he has been able to convey the concept of emotional intelligence to the world in simple language.

According to Reuven Bar-On (1997), 'emotional intelligence reflects one's ability to deal with daily environment challenges and helps predict one's success in life, including professional and personal pursuits'. Bar-On, a clinical psychologist with Trent University in Canada, is also said to have coined the term EQ, emotional quotient, in 1985 to describe his approach to assessing emotional intelligence. A growing body of research suggests that emotional intelligence as measured by emotional quotient is a better predictor of 'success' than the more traditional measures of intelligence quotient (IQ). Based on 17 years of research by him on over 33,000 individuals worldwide, he has developed the 'Bar-On Emotional Quotient Inventory' (EQ-i™) which measures emotional abilities such as self-regard, emotional self awareness, assertiveness, independence and self-actualisation, empathy, social responsibility, interpersonal relationship, reality testing, flexibility, problem-solving, stress tolerance, impulse control, optimism and happiness. Though Bar-On's claim of having collected data from more than 33,000 individuals is disputed by the scientific community, his coinage of the term 'EQ' is appreciated. But there is another

> Bar-On, coined the term EQ, i.e., emotional quotient, in 1985 to describe his approach to assessing emotional intelligence.

critical observation by the experts and researchers worldwide about his 'Emotional Quotient Test'. He has commercialised the concept of emotional intelligence by making the EQ test developed by him available on the Internet and elsewhere for a price, thus restricting its circulation among and evaluation by the scientific community.

Dalip Singh (2003) defines emotional intelligence as 'the ability of an individual to appropriately and successfully respond to a vast variety of emotional stimuli being elicited from the inner self and immediate environment. Emotional intelligence constitutes three psychological dimensions: emotional sensitivity, emotional maturity and emotional competency, all of which motivate an individual to recognise truthfully, interpret honestly and handle tactfully the dynamics of human behaviour'.

Let us discuss these three emotional factors in detail.

i. Emotional Competency

Managers have to master the following emotional competencies that have been identified after detailed research. These competencies are:

TACKLING EMOTIONAL UPSETS

This includes tackling frustrations, conflicts, inferiority complexes, etc. It also means avoiding emotional exhaustion such as stress, burnout and negativity of emotions. People in conflict are generally locked in a self-perpetuating emotional spiral in which the genesis of the conflict is usually not clear. Finding ways to deal with anger, fear, anxiety and sadness are essential signs of emotional competency. For example, learning how to manage yourself, when upset, is one such asset. Being able to channelise emotions to a positive end is another key skill to raise your EQ. Inferiority complex arising from issues such as knowledge, education, physical characteristics, religion, region, caste, sex and creed are not uncommon. Inferiority complex is also reflected in the low self-esteem, negative feelings and low opinion about oneself. Research shows that a high level of emotional intelligence helps overcome inferiority complex.

HIGH SELF-ESTEEM

Many managers often give themselves a negative feedback. On the other hand, there are those who believe that optimism can be a useful asset. Research conducted in Indian organisations has indicated that leaders should learn to be optimistic in order to boost their self-esteem. High self-esteem gives a manager realistic confidence to perceive challenges as learning opportunities, resulting in constant growth and improvement. High self-esteem is the greatest gift a manager can give to himself. Unfortunately, most of us suffer from a wounded self-esteem that often leads to a psychological invalidation of the self. Managers should learn and realise that high self-esteem is reflected in the feelings of confidence and competence.

TACTFUL RESPONSE TO EMOTIONAL STIMULI

This means being creative and practical towards emotional prompts elicited from the inner self and from the immediate environment. An emotionally intelligent manager will try to manipulate the on-going environment to his/her advantage by reacting appropriately.

HANDLING EGOISM

Egoism is based on the view that the fundamental motive behind all emotional conduct is self-interest. A self-centred manager talks incessantly about himself and his actions and is interested only in his own concerns. Tackling ego problems without hurting one's self-esteem is the key to success. An 'I am never wrong' attitude may be harmful in many situations. One should not be an egoist. It is the root cause of problems in interpersonal relations. Taking the initiative to resume dialogue and breaking the ice in situations where both parties have stuck to their original stand and have refused to budge, is a sign of emotional competency.

ii. Emotional Maturity

Emotional maturity is reflected in the behavioural pattern exhibited by managers while dealing with the inner self and the immediate environment. Let us now discuss some of the important aspects of emotional maturity.

SELF-AWARENESS

One of the basic emotional skills is the ability to recognise different feelings emanating from within and giving a name to them. Many managers are, in fact, unable to recognise their feelings and are therefore inclined to deny them. Knowing one's emotional strength and weaknesses is of great help because the inner self has to constantly respond to the outer world. It is generally believed that if one cannot interpret one's own emotions, he or she may not be able to do the same for others. This will reduce your effectiveness in handling interpersonal relationships.

DEVELOPING OTHERS

Recognising the value of contributions of others and encouraging their participation can often do good. Appreciating others' points of view and involving them actively in a project are signs of an emotionally intelligent manager. Unfortunately, we in India seem to lack this natural gift.

DELAYING GRATIFICATION

Managers may learn to delay gratification of reacting to a particular situation instantaneously. This helps to gain time to judge whether what is about to be said or done in the heat of the moment is the best course of action, by expressing personal concern without anger or passivity, and come out a winner. A manager must have plenty of patience and must not allow emotions to get the upper hand. Delaying gratification 'is doing right' and has far-reaching consequences in attaining success in personal and professional life.

ADAPTABILITY AND FLEXIBILITY

Knowing how and when to take the lead and when to follow are both essential emotional skills. Managers should know when to be aggressive and when to be passive. He should also know that there is a time to confront, withdraw, speak or remain silent. However, to do so, the manager has to control powerful negative tendencies such as jealousy, manipulation and the feeling of self-grandeur.

iii. Emotional Sensitivity

In the psychological sense, sensitivity means the characteristic of being peculiarly sensitive and judging the threshold for various types of stimulations, evoking sensations, feelings and emotions. Managers would gain much by developing the following personality traits.

UNDERSTANDING THE THRESHOLD OF EMOTIONAL AROUSAL

Managers should be in a position to respond to stimuli of low intensity. Equally important is the ability to be aware of the relationship between feelings and actions. What, for instance, triggered a particular emotion? What was the feeling behind a specific action? These are questions that managers ought to ask themselves to understand the intensity of emotions better.

EMPATHY

Empathy is the ability to sense how other people feel. It is the ability to share and accept another person's feelings. In India, we tend to call it the quality of humanness. It is the ability to listen to others without getting carried away by personal emotions. It is important to be able to distinguish between what others do or say, and one's own personal reactions and judgements. If you have empathy you will not hurt people; rather you will help them.

IMPROVING INTER-PERSONAL RELATIONS

Developing quality inter-relationships has a positive effect on all concerned. Positive inter-personal relations is a definite sign of success. The key to good inter-personal relations is to believe in the basic elements of trust, confidence and reliance. Research shows that the primary cause of failures among executives is their poor inter-personal relations at the workplace, resulting in stress and anxiety and lack of trust in others.

COMMUNICABILITY OF EMOTIONS

The influence of emotions is contagious and is communicated from one person to another instantaneously. A cheerful manager communicates a message of confidence and self-respect. In contrast, expressions of negative feeling by a manager communicate a message of pessimism, bitterness, suspicion and inferiority. Hence, managers should learn how to communicate positive emotions through verbal and non-verbal mediums.

A comparison of the EQ model based on definitions just discussed, is given below.

	Self-awareness	Self-management	Self-direction
Dalip Singh	Sensitivity	Maturity	Competency
Daniel Goleman	Know yourself	Choose yourself	Give yourself
Reuven Bar-On	Intra-personal	Inter-personal	Adaptability
Ester Orioli	Sense	Understand	Apply
Salovey, Mayer, Caruso	Perceive	Regulate	Generate

II. LEVELS OF EQ REQUIRED FOR VARIOUS JOBS

Martin Yate (1977), in his research, found that different jobs require different levels of EQ. It is now recognised that emotional intelligence plays an important role in many areas of life, including work. Researchers have examined the skills and aptitudes required to succeed in certain kinds of jobs. The role of emotional intelligence and the actual level of it required for various jobs, have also been examined. Jobs that can be accomplished individually or by working with others in fixed, set or structured ways do not require a great deal of emotional intelligence. Notwithstanding this, a high EQ can set you apart from your

> Some jobs require and some do not require a great deal of emotional intelligence.

colleagues and lead you to other forms of success at the workplace.

Jobs which demand interaction with other people, or working in informal teams, or empathising with and understanding others are the ones that require emotional intelligence. If you lack the requisite level of emotional intelligence, you may not only find such jobs difficult to cope with, but also less satisfying.

Bosses and leaders, in particular, should have high EQ because they represent the organisation, they interact with the largest number of people within and outside the organisation and they set the tone for employee morale. Leaders high on empathy are able to understand their employees' needs and provide them with constructive feedback.

Different jobs also call for different types of emotional intelligence. For example, success in sales requires the empathic ability to gauge a customer's mood and the interpersonal skill to decide when to pitch a product and when to keep quiet. In contrast, success in painting or professional tennis requires a more individual form of self-discipline and motivation.

TABLE 5.1: Level of EQ Required for Various Jobs
(From low to high EQ)

Biochemist (lowest)	Librarian
Chef	EEG Technologist
Billing Clerk	Consultant
Forester	Broker
Systems Analyst	Radiological Technician
Electrical Engineer	Dental Hygienist
Mechanical Engineer	Benefits/Compensation Analyst
Auditor	Retail Sales Associate
Underwriter	Fireman
Accountant	Environmental Lawyer
Geophysicist	Writer
Geneticist	Environmental Educator
MIS Manager	Dentist
Software Engineer	Police Officer
Chemical Engineer	Nurse Aide
Civil Engineer	Nurse/Occupational Therapist

Contd.

Contd.

Restaurant Manager	Recreational Therapist
Waiter/Waitress	Training Manager
Medical Assistant	Adult Education Teacher
Medical Secretary	Public Relations Professional
Dental Laboratory Technician	Nurse
Travel Agent	Human Resources Manager
Controller	Teacher
Paralegal	Physical Therapist
Secretary	Psychiatric Aide
Medical Record Technician	Special Education Teacher
Optician	Family Medical Doctor
Loan Officer	Internist
Insurance Agent	Geriatric Care Specialist
Editor	MSW/Social Worker
Sales Representative	Human Services Worker
Urban Planner	Psychiatry (Highest)

Yate listed various jobs on the basis of the level of emotional intelligence they require for success and satisfaction (see Table 5.1). It is clear from this list that a psychiatrist requires the highest level of EQ to deal with clients as compared to a botanist, who may require a lower level of it. EQ and success in various professions and jobs have been studied and compiled by the Consortium for Research on Emotional Intelligence in Organisations. The first study undertaken in a major Asian bank compared the EQ and IQ of a group of people and measured their work performance.

III. EMOTIONAL INTELLIGENCE COMPETENCIES

R. Boyatzis et al. (2000) have described a model of emotional intelligence competencies that reflect four domains: (*a*) self-awareness, (*b*) self-management, (*c*) social awareness and (*d*) relationship management. The model appears more theoretical as its applications in practical situations have not been tested. It would definitely add more value to the model, as shown in Table 5.2, if it is tested in real-life situations and the results made known. The framework presents 20 competencies that nest in four clusters of general emotional intelligence abilities. The framework illustrates, for example, that we cannot demonstrate competencies of trustworthiness and conscientiousness without mastery of the fundamental ability of self-management or the competencies of influence, communication, conflict management, and so on, without a handle on managing relationships.

TABLE 5.2: Framework of Emotional Competencies

	Self Personal Competence	Other Social Competence
Recognition	**Self-Awareness** • Emotional self-awareness • Accurate self-assessment • Self-confidence	**Social Awareness** • Empathy • Service orientation • Organisational awareness
Regulation	**Self-Management** • Self-control • Trustworthiness • Conscientiousness • Adaptability • Achievement drive • Initiative	**Relationship Management** • Developing others • Influence • Communication • Conflict management • Leadership • Change catalyst • Building bonds • Teamwork & collaboration

These clusters are discussed in detail in the following sections.

i. The Self-Awareness Cluster

This cluster deals with the understanding of feelings and accurate self-assessment, and comprises three competencies relating to performance at the workplace.

EMOTIONAL SELF-AWARENESS

It reflects the importance of recognising one's feelings and how they affect one's performance. At a financial services company, emotional self-awareness proved crucial in financial planners' job performance.

ACCURATE SELF-ASSESSMENT

At another level, self-awareness is the key to realising one's strengths and weaknesses. Among several hundred managers from 12 different organisations, accurate self-assessment was the hallmark of superior performance. Individuals with the accurate competence in self-assessment are aware of their abilities and limitations, seek out feedback and learn from their mistakes, and know where they need to improve and when to work with others who have complementary strengths.

SELF-CONFIDENCE

A high degree of self-confidence among supervisors, managers, and executives, distinguishes the best from the average performer.

ii. The Self-Management Cluster

This cluster refers to managing internal states, impulses and resources, and includes six competencies relating to workplace performance.

EMOTIONAL SELF-CONTROL

Heading the list is competence in emotional self-control, which manifests largely as the absence of distress and disruptive feelings. Signs of this competence include being unfazed in stressful situations or dealing with a hostile person without lashing out in return.

TRUSTWORTHINESS

Trustworthiness competence translates into letting others know one's values and principles, intentions and feelings, and acting in ways that are consistent with them. Trustworthy individuals are forthright about their own mistakes and confront others about their lapses. Deficiency in this ability can derail a career.

CONSCIENTIOUSNESS

The signs of conscientiousness competence include being careful, self-disciplined and scrupulous in attending to responsibilities.

ADAPTABILITY

If there is any single competence our present times call for, it is adaptability. Superior performers in management ranks exhibit this competence.

ACHIEVEMENT ORIENTATION

This is the competence that drives success of entrepreneurs. In its most general sense, this competence, also known as achievement drive, refers to an optimistic striving to continually improve performance.

INITIATIVE

Those with strong initiative competence act before being forced to do so by external events. This often means taking anticipatory action to avoid problems before they happen, or taking advantage of opportunities before they are visible to anyone else.

iii. The Social Awareness Cluster

This cluster refers to reading people and groups accurately, and encompasses three competencies relating to performance at work.

EMPATHY

Empathy competence gives people an astute awareness of others' emotions, concerns and needs. The empathic individual can read emotional currents, picking up on nonverbal cues such as tone of voice or facial expression.

SERVICE

The ability to identify a client's or customer's often-unstated needs and concerns and then match them to products or services is an individual's service competence. This empathic strategy distinguishes star sales performers from average ones. It also means taking a long-term perspective, sometimes trading off immediate gains in order to preserve customer relationships.

ORGANISATIONAL AWARENESS

The ability to read currents of emotions and political realities in groups is a competence vital to behind-the-scenes networking and coalition building that allows individuals to wield influence, no matter what their professional role.

iv. The Relationship Management Cluster

This cluster refers to inducing desirable responses in others and has 12 competencies relating to performance at work.

DEVELOPING OTHERS
Developing others involves sensing people's developmental needs and bolstering their abilities—a talent not just of excellent coaches and mentors, but also outstanding leaders.

INFLUENCE
We practice the essence of influence competence when we handle and manage emotions effectively in other people and are persuasive. The most effective people sense others' reactions and fine-tune their own responses to move interaction in the best direction.

COMMUNICATION
Creating an atmosphere of openness, with clear lines of communication, is a key factor in organisational success. People who exhibit communication competence are effective in the give-and-take of emotional information, deal with difficult issues in a straightforward manner, listen well and welcome sharing information, and foster open communication and stay receptive to bad news as well as good.

CONFLICT MANAGEMENT
Effective conflict management and negotiation are important to long-term, symbiotic business relationships, such as those between manufacturers and retailers. In a survey of retail buyers in department store chains, effectiveness at win–win negotiating was an accurate barometer of the health of the manufacturer–retailer relationship.

VISIONARY LEADERSHIP
Those adept at visionary leadership competence draw on a range of personal skills to inspire others to work together towards common

goals. They are able to articulate and arouse enthusiasm for a shared vision and mission, step forward as needed, guide the performance of others while holding them accountable and lead by example.

CHANGE CATALYST

An effective change leader articulates a compelling vision of new organisational goals. A leader's competence at catalysing change brings greater efforts and better performance from subordinates, making their work more effective.

BUILDING BONDS

Competence in building bonds epitomises stars in fields like engineering, computer science, biotechnology, and other *knowledge work* fields in which networking is crucial for success. These stars tend to choose people with a particular expertise or resource to be part of their networks.

COLLABORATION AND TEAMWORK

Collaboration and teamwork competence has taken on increased importance in the last decade with the trend toward team-based work in many organisations. Teamwork itself depends on the collective emotional intelligence of its members; the most productive teams are those that exhibit emotional intelligence competencies at the team level.

Although there is theoretical significance in showing that each competence in itself has a significant impact on performance, it is also in a sense an artificial exercise. In life, and particularly on the job, people exhibit these competencies in groupings, often across clusters, and allow competencies to support one another. Emotional competencies seem to operate most powerfully in synergistic groupings, with evidence suggesting that mastery of a 'critical mass' of competencies is necessary for superior performance. Organisations and individuals interface in ways that require a multitude of emotional intelligence abilities, each most effective when used in conjunction with others. Emotional self-control, for instance, supports empathy and influence competencies. Finding a comfortable fit between an individual and an organisation is easier when important aspects of organisational culture (rapid growth, for example) link to a grouping of competencies rather than to any one. Competencies operate together in an integrated fashion, forming a meaningful pattern of abilities that facilitate successful performance in a given role or job. However, the model of emotional intelligence competency framework has its share of criticism that its propagators need to address at once through future research.

IV. EQ IN THE INDIAN PERSPECTIVE

Dalip Singh (2003) has, after empirical study, arrived at a definition of emotional intelligence in the Indian perspective. Research on human behaviour in Indian homes and organisations has shown that the Indian family is a closely-knit entity with visible emotional bonding. The members of the family are interdependent, not only economically and socially, but also emotionally. The bonding is unlimited and everlasting. When Indians go abroad, they experience an uncontrolled emotional craving for their family and homeland. The emotional bonds may be seen in the relationship between husband and wife, parents and children and also between children.

> The Indian family is a closely-knit entity with visible emotional bonding.

Similarly, Indian business also reflects an emotional environment. The elements of bonding in the family are carried over to the workplace and may be felt from the relationship between an employer and the employee. Unlike in developed countries, Indian business is yet to adopt a thoroughly professional approach that is usually characterised by impersonal relations, devoid of emotions. Indian business is still dominated by a family environment and is run on emotional ties. The commitment to business or family business is wholesome, unchallenged and undisputed. This results in a semi-permanent emotional commitment of employees to work in an organisation for their entire life. The Indian executive's personality reflects a distinctive management style that is more empathetic, understanding, non-manipulative and benevolent. The

Indian executive normally stays on in one organisation for long periods and job-hopping is not very common in the country. The Indian management style revolves around our cultural roots and upbringing. An Indian grows up in a system where family ties and the sense of belonging get top priority. Coming from such an environment of strong family ties, an youngster gets a shock when he grows up and sees the job environment practicing management philosophies which he cannot identify with at all. The bonding that he or she is used to, either does not exist or are not as strong in developed countries like the US and the EU. For example, the most common contradiction in management styles between America and India is that the former has a contractual style of management and the latter has a lifetime employment concept. The US-based industrial environment is based on a hire-and-fire system that ignores emotional commitment of employers and employees towards each other. The American system, for obvious reasons, is repugnant to the bond-loving Indians.

It may also be appreciated that the emotional set-up in Indian society is completely different from that in the US, Europe and other developed societies. One may generalise by saying that Indians are more emotional as compared with their counterparts in developed countries. A recent research of successful Indians there tells us that they are not necessarily the happiest people. The India-centric approach proves that most Indians value emotional bonds and long-term relationships. However, shockingly enough, well-known Indian management institutions have not been able to come out of the various complexes that they suffer from. They are still proud of the fact that their faculty has been trained in an American institute without recognising that the American management style is not suited to Indian conditions. None claim that their faculty has done research on Indian management and is trying to find out what is good for Indian corporates. This is a modern management paradox that needs to be addressed at once.

Many experts worldwide have attempted to define emotional intelligence. Interestingly, most of the research work on this subject has been carried out in the US, with some stray research findings in Europe and Canada. The concept of emotional intelligence has originated from the US. Hence, the concept is unwittingly favourably inclined towards the US population. The emotional characteristics or emotional competencies being considered as essential are, therefore, more close to the heart of the US due to the culture bias. The Consortium for Research on Emotional Intelligence in Organisations is probably the only organisation in the world that has taken the responsibility to carry out quality research on emotional intelligence. The majority of literature and research is also US-based with very little work being done elsewhere. Hence, on the basis of limited research, can we conclude that the components of emotional intelligence as being propagated by American researchers are exhaustive? Can we include some more psychological inputs or remove some? Are the psychological characteristics, identified by researchers as the components of emotional intelligence, universal? Are these culture-specific? Can emotional intelligence be defined in any other way? Do we need to take a fresh look and have a culture-specific definition of emotional intelligence reflecting the Indian psyche? To answer some of these questions it was decided to conduct an empirical study and determine the concept of emotional intelligence keeping in view the Indian perspective.

A national-level interactive workshop was organised by the PHD Chamber of Commerce and Industry in New Delhi on 16 August 2002 to discuss the theme 'Emotional Intelligence at Work'. Established in 1905, PHDCCI today is an apex business chamber in India that has actively served trade and industry for more than nine decades. It has around 1,500 direct members including corporate entities from large, medium and small-scale sectors, export houses and professionals. Through its 112 association members, the chamber reaches out to 35,000 small-scale units. Offering varied services in tune with the requirements of its constituents, the chamber provides a common platform for meetings of representatives of trade, business and industry with senior government officials at the central and state levels, and plays an important role in the formulation of government policies. The PHDCCI is a premium national industrial body of industrialist, businessmen entrepreneurs and institutions in India. The Chamber believes in the philosophy of progress, harmony and development of Indian business, and organises interactive workshops, seminars and discussions on important contemporary issues relating to HRD, personnel management and entrepreneurship development. The participants in the EQ seminar included more than 100 chief executives and managing directors of leading Indian business organisations. Among others, psychologists from University of Delhi, Punjab University, Chandigarh, and Kurukshetra University, Kurukshetra, Haryana, were also invited. It was an open house interactive discussion together with a technical session on 'Emotional Intelligence at Work'. Professor N.K. Chadha of University of Delhi, who has developed the popular EQ test in collaboration with the author for the Indian population, administered the test to the participants and provided its scoring and interpretation on the spot. Dr Singh, the author, explained the concept of emotional intelligence and its various ramifications in professional and personal life.

After the discussions, there was consensus among the participants that the definition(s) provided by American psychologists had a definite cultural bias. It was thought appropriate to evolve a new definition of emotional intelligence and its psychological characteristics, and have an entirely fresh look at the construct validity of the concept. It was felt that emotional characteristics, as defined by psychologists worldwide, did not cover the whole range of human behaviour and its reactions to divergent stimuli in day-to-day life. It was argued that the Indian context required a specific cultural, social, psychological and behavioural definition based on its distinct cultural and social milieu to explain the concept of emotional intelligence. The use of the term 'emotional intelligence' to depict certain feelings, moods and behaviours also came under attack and it was felt that a more appropriate definition of emotional intelligence may be evolved in the Indian context.

Keeping in view this background, the psychological experts present at the workshop wanted to know from the participants what, they 'felt', constitutes emotional intelligence. This was thought necessary in order to establish a construct validity of the concept of emotional intelligence. At the end of the workshop, the participants were given a question that they had to answer on the spot. The participants were told to keep in mind the broad concept of emotional intelligence, the scores they had obtained on the EQ test administered to them, and their personal feelings of internal and external environment of self and work while answering the question given below:

> **Question:** *What components/characteristics/traits do you FEEL (not think) constitute emotional intelligence? Please indicate FIVE choices:*
>
> Answers:
>
> 1. _____
>
> 2. _____
>
> 3. _____
>
> 4. _____
>
> 5. _____
>
> Name _____ (optional)
>
> Profession/Class _____
>
> Age _____
>
> Sex _____ M _____ F _____
>
> Date and place _____

The experts also decided to seek responses to the same question from postgraduate and undergraduate university students who had a reasonably good knowledge and exposure to psychology as a subject, in order to determine what they felt about the concept. The sample and its characteristics are given in Table 5.3.

TABLE 5.3: Study on Postgraduate and Undergraduate Students

Sr. No.	Sample Description	Sample Size	Institution Studied
1.	CEOs/Entrepreneurs/Industrialists	74	PHD Chamber of Commerce and Industry, New Delhi
2.	Postgraduate students	42	Department of Psychology, University of Delhi
3.	Postgraduate students	26	Department of Psychology, Punjab University, Chandigarh
4.	Postgraduate students	20	Faculty of Management Studies, University of Delhi
5.	Postgraduate students	15	Management Development Institute, Gurgaon, Haryana
6.	Postgraduate students	23	Department of Psychology, Kurukshetra University, Haryana
7.	Postgraduate students	20	Department of Psychology, MDU University, Rohtak
8.	Postgraduate students	22	Department of Computer Application, Haryana Technical University, Hissar
9.	Graduate students	25	Department of Psychology, Government College, Sector 46, Chandigarh
10.	Graduate students	25	Institute of Management Education, Sahibabad, Uttar Pradesh
11.	Graduate students	30	Faculty of Commerce, Delhi School of Economics, University of Delhi
	Total	**322**	

Later, a team of experts on psychological testing from University of Delhi, Defence Institute of Psychological Research, Ministry of Defence, Government of India, and Department of Psychology, Punjab University, Chandigarh, tabulated the responses. The responses obtained were 'tally marked' to obtain the frequency and percentage of responses, in order to identify the dimensions constituting emotional intelligence. As may be seen, the sample was collected from 322 subjects from different institutions, and the total number of responses obtained was 1,610 (322 × 5). After content validly analysis by the experts, these responses were found to constitute four major dimensions, as shown in Table 5.4.

TABLE 5.4: Frequency of Response

Sr. No.	Dimensions	Frequency of Responses	Percentage
1	Emotional competency	545	33.85
2	Emotional maturity	450	27.95
3	Emotional sensitivity	375	23.30
4	Others/Invalid*	240*	14.90*
	Total	**1610**	**100.00**

* It may be seen that 240 responses (14.90 per cent) were not considered as these were found to have a variance of 1 to 3 per cent only, and therefore declared invalid. Some of the responses in this dimension were family background, mental phenomena, putting in hard work, perceiving emotions, will power, rational thinking, social interaction and knowledge sharing.

The responses to the test discussed are shown in graphic form in Figure 5.1.

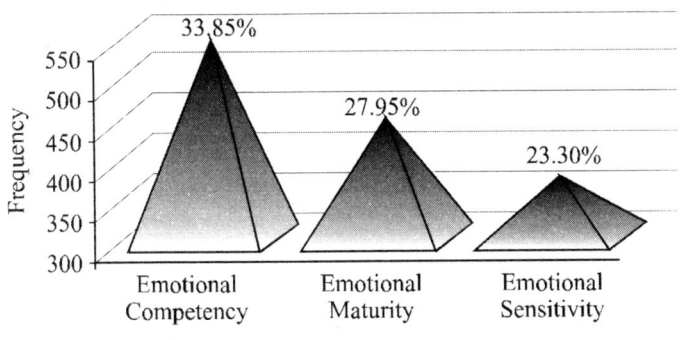

FIGURE 5.1: Dimensions of Emotional Intelligence

The analysis further shows that three dimensions have been identified, with frequency ranging from 375 to 545 and 85 per cent of the variance being explained by them. Based on these findings, *emotional competency* (33.85 per cent), *emotional maturity* (27.95 per cent) and *emotional sensitivity* (23.30 per cent) have emerged as the key dimensions constituting emotional intelligence.

- **Emotional Competency** The capacity to tactfully respond to emotional stimuli elicited by various situations; having

high self-esteem and optimism; communication skills; ability to tackle emotional upsets such as frustration, conflicts, egoism and inferiority complexes; enjoying emotions; doing what succeeds; ability to relate to others; emotional self-control; capacity to avoid emotional exhaustion such as stress and burnout and learning to avoid negativity of emotions.
- **Emotional Maturity** The ability to evaluate emotions of oneself and others; identify and express feelings; balance the state of heart and mind; appreciate others' points of view; develop others; delay gratification of immediate psychological satisfaction; and being adaptable and flexible.
- **Emotional Sensitivity** Constitutes understanding the threshold of emotional arousal; managing the immediate environment; maintaining rapport, harmony and comfort with others and letting others feel comfortable in your company. It also involves being honest in interpersonal dealings; interpreting emotional cues truthfully; realising communicability of emotions, moods and feelings; and having an insight into how others evaluate and relate to you.

These dimensions of emotional intelligence are presented diagrammatically in Figure 5.2.

Based on the above empirical process, the following operational definition is proposed by the author in the Indian context:

Emotional intelligence is the ability of an individual to appropriately and successfully respond to a vast variety of emotional stimuli being elicited from

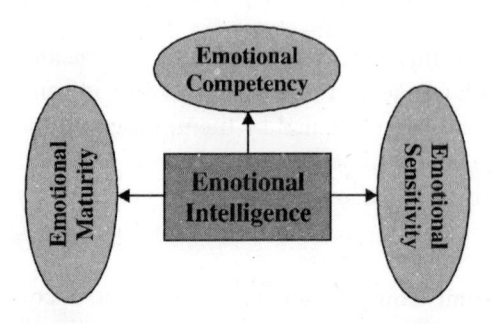

FIGURE 5.2: Defining Emotional Intelligence

the inner self and immediate environment. Emotional intelligence constitutes three psychological dimensions: emotional sensitivity, emotional maturity and emotional competency, which motivate an individual to recognise truthfully, interpret honestly and handle tactfully the dynamics of human behaviour.

This operational definition refers to certain terms that require interpretation. *Ability* refers to the conscious emotional effort by an individual to adapt to the environment; *emotional stimuli* means prompts from the inner self and the immediate environment; *motivate* means how behaviour gets satisfied, energised, sustained and directed to achieve desired goals; *appropriately* means a right mixture of heart and head, i.e., pros and cons of a particular emotional reaction; *success* means to do what one has tried or waited to do with a favourable result; *tactfully* means being creative and practical.

As a clinical psychologist, I refer to my model of emotional intelligence as a 'theory of personality', though some recent researchers prefer to term it as a 'theory of performance' by making a business case out of it. The personality theories as established by Hans Eysenck, Alfred Adler, Carl Jung, B.F. Skinner, Gordon Allport, Sigmund Freud, Abraham Maslow and other legends in this field, have concluded that 'personality consists of those permanent and semi-permanent modes of behaviour which characterise an individual and make him or her different from other people'. These individual differences are called 'traits'—sociability, persistence, impulsiveness, suggestibility, pride and humility, and so on. Certain personality traits usually correlate with others. We know, for example, that people who are sociable are often impulsive, venturesome, physically active and talkative as well.

The relationship between traits gives rise to the higher concept of personality 'types'. One such type dimension is 'extroversion and introversion' with extreme extrovert characterised by sociability, impulsiveness, ventureness, outgoing nature, etc.; and introverts being exactly the opposite. Another dimension of personality is that of emotionality and stability. Psychologists believe that though many dimensions of personality traits and types are strongly determined by genetic factors, the emotionality dimension is, however, relatively less influenced by genetic factors and more by the limbic system of the brain. Hormones too are intimately related to the emotional-stability dimension of a personal. Hence, it may be appreciated that affective, non-affective or emotional aspects of an individual's life were always a part of the definitions of personality. 'Emotions' are an integral part of personality; so is 'intelligence'. Psychologists studying personality have empirically found that 'intelligence' is the foremost trait of the personality of an individual. Hence, any discussion on emotional intelligence cannot be treated as valid if is does not specifically refer to the theories of personality. You cannot de-link intelligence from personality. While elaborating on the concept of emotional intelligence, a discussion on personality is but obvious. Let us conclude by saying that the origin of the term 'intelligence' is from 'personality theories' and the origin of the term 'emotional intelligence' is from 'intelligence' as defined in the personality theories. Intelligence is an area of personality that is usually treated apart from other aspects although it interacts closely with the personality traits and types. A very intelligent extrovert, for example, is very different from a dull extrovert.

V. Do Different Professions Require Different Levels of EQ?

In yet another research, Dalip Singh (2003) attempted to find out if different professions required different levels of emotional intelligence. The salient features of the research paper are produced below.

Introduction This research has been carried out by Singh (2003) to test the hypothesis that different professions may exhibit different levels of emotional intelligence. Goleman (1996) defines emotional intelligence as knowing what feels good, what feels bad, and how to go from bad to good. It includes emotional awareness and emotional management of skills that provide the ability to balance emotion and reason so as

> The researcher's hypothesis is that different professions require different levels of emotional intelligence.

to maximise one's long-term happiness. Emotional intelligence includes components such as self-awareness, the ability to manage moods, motivation and empathy, and social skills such as cooperation and leadership. It is believed that learning difficulties and problems of maladjustment at the workplace have their origin in poorly developed emotional awareness in early childhood. Emotions enable human beings to respond appropriately to a variety of environmental situations. In today's business world, management pundits have always wondered whether different professions exhibit different emotional intelligence levels or not. Some professions may exhibit a great deal of emotional intelligence while others may not.

There are professions that require interacting with people, working in teams or having informal relationships. For example, leaders may need a higher degree of EQ because of the very nature of their job, which requires them to interact with a large number of people, and empathise and understand their needs and desires. Experience shows that success in sales requires an ability to judge clients' moods and the emotional skill to decide when to promote the product and when to keep quiet. Such professions may be satisfying only when one has the requisite level of emotional intelligence. In contrast, jobs that can be executed individually in structured or fixed ways may not require a great deal of emotional intelligence. For instance, success in painting or professional tennis may require more self-discipline and motivation, and less EQ. The researcher's hypothesis is that different professions require different emotional levels.

The emotional competence of a person is a learned capability that leads to outstanding performance at work. It is believed that emotional intelligence determines the potential to learn practical skills that are based on the five elements of *self-awareness, motivation, self-regulation, empathy* and *adeptness in relationships*. The emotional competence of a person shows how much of his potential is translated into on-the-job capabilities. For example, providing good customer service is an emotional competence based on empathy. Similarly, trustworthiness is a competence based on self-regulation or handling impulses and emotions well. Both customer service and trustworthiness are competencies that can lead to outstanding performance in certain professions. However, simply having a high level of emotional intelligence does not necessarily guarantee that a person will be professionally successful. A person may be high on empathy but he may not have acquired the skills based on empathy that lead to superior customer service, the ability to coach or monitor staff, or the ability to bring together a diverse team. Similarly, self-awareness, optimism and empathy may be more relevant to other professions. Hence, emotional and personal competencies are vital for certain professions. The workplace is the ideal setting for the promotion of these emotional competencies. Some professions have realised that emotional abilities hold the key to a successful career and they are now showing greater interest in developing these abilities.

Before we move ahead it is necessary to define 'success'. The word may have different meanings for different people. So, what is 'success'? Is it to reach top positions at the workplace? Is it being rich and wealthy? Is it being powerful, dominating or influential? Is it occupying senior positions in the bureaucracy? It is a relative term.

Most of us assume we know what success is. But is there a standard definition for the word? Synonyms for the word 'successful' include prosperous, flourishing, thriving, prospering, booming, growing, mushrooming, fruitful, lucrative and advancing. But the problem is how do you measure and quantify success? For example, a professional may consider himself to be successful when he reaches the top position in his organisation. On the contrary, a housewife may consider herself successful if she leads a satisfying personal life. While selecting the subjects from various professions for the present study, it was never our intention to categorise the subjects as 'successful' or otherwise. The subjects were chosen keeping in mind variables such as experience, seniority, standing in the profession and turnover in the business, in order to make the sample representative.

Objective The objective of the present study was to ascertain empirically whether different professions require different levels of emotional intelligence or not. Further, the aim was to grade the professions in descending order of EQ.

Methodology Before taking up the study, it was thought necessary to define 'profession'. According to the Longman Dictionary of Contemporary English, a profession 'is a form of employment especially the one that is possible for educated persons after training such as law, medicine or teaching, and that is respected in society as honourable and include the whole body of people in a particular profession and reflects one's belief, opinion or feeling'. Based on this definition, various professions were selected for the study. It may be pertinent to point out that the professions selected for the study pre-supposed a high level of intelligence quotient (IQ) among them. This is due to the fact that these professions require passing difficult exams and obtaining degrees, diplomas and high academic pass percentages. The EQ test developed by Chadha (2001) was used to collect data. The test, which contains 15 situations measuring different emotional responses and their blends, has been standardised for Indian managers, businessmen, and bureaucrats. The retest reliability for the test was found to be 0.94. The split-half reliability in the case of odd-even items was 0.92 and that for the first half and the second half was 0.90. Both reliability coefficients are significantly higher which indicate that the present scale is highly consistent and reliable. The empirical validity of the scale was calculated by administering the scale of Daniel Goleman and present scale to a sample of 60 subjects. The validity was found to be 0.89, which indicates that the present scale is valid.

Let us see a sample situation given in the test relating to the police profession and measuring empathy and tactfulness. *Imagine that you are a police officer posted in a sensitive area. You get the information that there have been violent ethnic clashes between two religious communities and a large number of people have been killed from both sides and property damaged. What action will you take?* (*a*) Decide not to visit spot personally as there may be a danger to your life. (*b*) Take your time to responding any case this is not the first time riots have occurred. (*c*) Try to handle the situation tactfully by assuaging the feelings of both communities, tracking down the reasons for clash, and taking all desired remedial measures. (*d*) Send your subordinate inspector to study the situation. (*e*) Arrange to hand over the dead to the respective families after getting the postmortem done.

A list of 27 professions was drawn up by four experts in psychology from Punjab University, Chandigarh. It was decided to study as many professions as possible. After analysing various professions on the basis of emotional intelligence required, job requirements, job profile, stress experienced, and internal and external psychological factors, these experts decided to retain 18 professions in the present study. The professions deleted by the experts were army, navy, air force, para-military, post and telegraph, forest, library, fire service and writing. The experts felt these professions might require a separate study due to their entirely varied nature of work and the emotional competencies required. Since the sample involved subjects from different professions at a fairly senior level, it was decided to use the non-probability sampling technique which requires that there is no way of estimating the probability that each element has an equal chance of being included in the sample. This technique is characterised by collecting data from the first available individual of the population. The experts of psychological testing also suggested that a minimum of 15 subjects be included in the study from each profession to have reliable and valid results. However, there was no restriction on the maximum number of subjects in each profession. Once the sample, its nature and number of subjects were finalised, the data collection process was taken up. The EQ test was explained to the subjects, instructions read out and the test was administered. Individual care was taken to establish rapport with the subjects and only willing participants were asked to fill up the questionnaire. The subjects were assured full confidentiality. A team of six postgraduate students from the psychology department of Punjab University, Chandigarh, who had sufficient experience in conducting similar research, collected the dataover a period of 60 days on different dates and times. A total of 395 questionnaires were distributed out of which 354 were returned. Seven questionnaires were rejected as these were found to be incomplete giving a sample size of 347.

The 18 professions covered in the study were: artists (persons associated with dance, drama and acting), insurance (officers of nationalised insurance companies), advertising (persons managing advertising agencies), social work (NGOs, Red Cross Society, Child

Welfare Society), teaching (university teachers), legal (advocates), tourism (managers of recognised tourist agencies), politics (members of legislative assemblies), business/entrepreneurship (persons having their own business with a turnover of more than Rs 5 crore a year), police (Indian Police Service officers), judiciary (sub judge and above), administration (Indian Administrative Service officers), information technology (computer programmers, software engineers), medicine (MBBS doctors), banking (managers and assistant managers), engineering (executive engineers and above), accountancy (chartered accountants having a standing of more than five years in the profession), and nursing (para-medical staff).

Results The results obtained on subjects are presented in Table 5.5 in descending order:

TABLE 5.5: The Results

Sr. No.	Name of Profession	Number of Subjects	Average EQ Scores from High to Low	Interpretation	Standard Deviation
1	Artist	15	290	Extremely high	5.7
2	Insurance	25	285	Extremely high	17.5
3	Advertisement	20	285	Extremely high	11.5
4	Social work	15	285	Extremely high	31.8
5	Teaching	20	280	High	23.5
6	Legal	25	260	High	8.9
7	Tourism	22	255	High	14.6
8	Politics	15	255	High	8.2
9	Business/Entrepreneurship	15	255	High	16.8
10	Police	25	250	High	26.7
11	Judiciary	15	245	Average	5.5
12	Administration	25	215	Average	7.4
13	Information Technology	15	210	Average	11.6
14	Medicine	20	210	Average	14.5
15	Banking	20	200	Average	23.4
16	Engineering	20	200	Average	7.3
17	Accountancy	20	195	Average	27.9
18	Nursing	15	185	Average	14.0

Further, the data was subjected to Cluster Analysis to find cluster of professions having homogeneity on EQ scores. For this purpose, basic data was analysed with the help of the correlational analyses technique and then Holzinger B-coefficient of belongingness was used to get various clusters. The correlational matrix obtained was 18 ? 18 for the purpose of subjecting it to cluster analyses and formulating the appropriate clusters based on the B-coefficient technique. Based on the above statistical analysis, the following clusters (as shown in Table 5.6) were formulated:

TABLE 5.6: Clusters and Professions

Clusters	Professions Included	Interpretation
Cluster I	Artist, Insurance, Advertisement, Social work	Extremely high
Cluster II	Teaching, Legal, Tourism, Politics, Business/Entrepreneurship, Police	High
Cluster III	Judiciary, Administration, Information Technology, Medicine, Banking, Engineering, Accountancy, Nursing	Average

The cluster analysis clearly reveals that all the 18 professions can be clustered into three clusters. The first cluster constitutes four professions exhibiting an extremely high EQ level—artist, insurance, advertisement and social work. This means that with reference to EQ these professions are similar. This probably indicates that one needs to have an extremely high degree of EQ to achieve job satisfaction in these professions. The second cluster consists of six professions: teaching, legal, tourism, politics, business/entrepreneurship and police. The professions in this cluster are homogeneous in nature and show a kind of commonality. To be 'successful' in any of these professions, one needs a high EQ level. The third cluster constitutes eight professions exhibiting average EQ: judiciary, administration, information technology, medicine, banking, engineering, accountancy and nursing. In these professions, individuals with moderate EQ can also perform effectively.

The above EQ scores have been presented in a bar diagram in Figure 5.3.

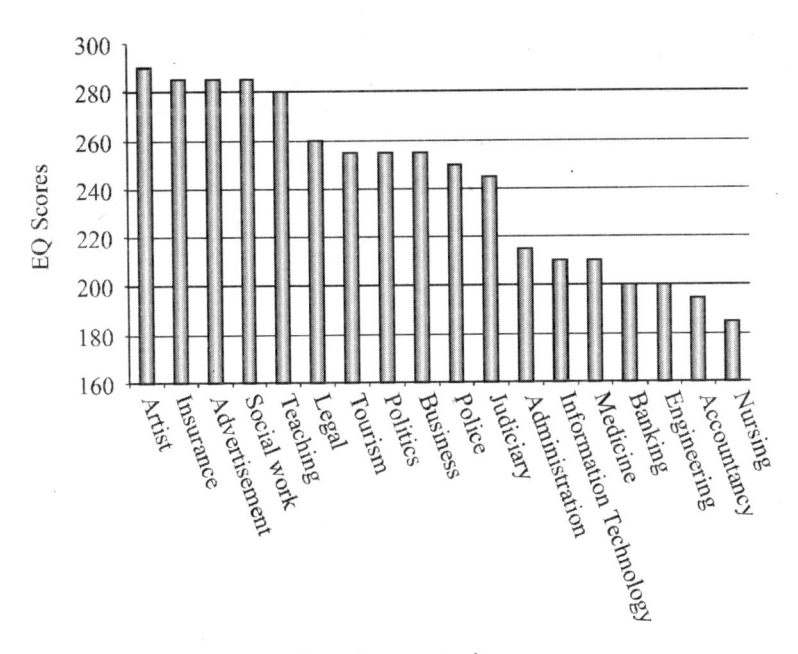

FIGURE 5.3: Professions

Discussion In the first cluster are some professions that require one to consolidate one's emotional skills. People in the first cluster—artist, insurance, advertisement and social work—may need to express feelings, identify and label feelings and manage and control impulses. That is exactly the reason why EQ scores of these professions are found to be extremely high. These professions may also require interpreting emotional cues that may influence social behaviour. These emotional competencies may help them in problem solving and decision-making. These are also the professions that require use of non-verbal skills such as communicating through eye contact, facial expression, and tone of voice or gestures. For example, it is the job of an insurance salesperson to approach prospective clients to sell insurance policies. Experience shows that a number of people slam the door on the salespersons' faces, resulting in a feeling of acute frustration. It is, therefore, understandable that this profession requires an extremely high level of EQ to help an insurance salesman re-access his/her capabilities and evolve fresh strategies to overcome similar feelings in the future. An insurance salesperson, therefore, needs to be an optimist, an important emotional competence and one with high EQ will take failure as a challenge without getting demoralised. A US-based national insurance company has also found that salesmen who were weak in emotional competencies such as self confidence, initiative and empathy sold policies with an average premium of US $54,000 only, but those very strong on these emotional competencies sold policies with premiums worth US $114,000.

In the second cluster, are professions that require a high level of EQ. For example, the teaching profession requires emotional competencies such as rapport, harmony and comfort while dealing with groups. A teacher with high IQ may not necessarily be high in these emotional competencies. Hence, teachers with high EQ seem to exhibit open and free expression of ideas that lead them to creativity and mutual respect. In the police profession, a person has to constantly work under stress emanating from threat to life, while encountering criminal elements and dealing with communal clashes. The police officer is expected to handle the situation tactfully and the job requires firmness and empathy in appropriate doses. A police officer with high EQ knows how to manage emotions of people, emotions of victims in difficult times such as ethnic clashes, rape, political demonstrations and student strikes. Political leaders, as well as successful businessmen/entrepreneurs, advocates, and the people engaged in tourism are supposed to be high on EQ.

The remaining eight professions in the third cluster—judiciary, administration, information technology, medicine, banking, engineering, accountancy and nursing—have obtained average scores in the EQ test. This is indicative of a trend that these professions may not require a high degree EQ. In other words, a moderate level of EQ appears to be sufficient to be successful in these professions. Bureaucrats, for instance, display average EQ scores, and need to have self-confidence, motivation and the ability to manage emotions. At the same time, they face conflict, stress and burnout from internal and external factors. These findings show that IAS officers with moderate EQ can deal with situations effectively. The judiciary also displays a moderate EQ score. The field of information technology needs a dedicated and individualistic approach at the workplace. The software engineer, computer programmer or computer engineer has to concentrate on programmes that require minimal interaction with people. Hence, it is not surprising that the study has thrown up an average EQ scores in these professions. Other researchers have also found that scientists, engineers and IT professionals may prove to be effective in their professions even with a moderate amount of EQ. Similarly, in medicine, banking, engineering and accountancy professions, the job is entirely impersonal, involving monetary transactions and financial matters that usually have little or no interaction with people. In financial institutions, rules and regulations are well defined and cannot be changed or modified. Hence, an average EQ is fine in these professions.

We may conclude by saying that different professions do require different levels of EQ. However, having a high or average EQ cannot simplistically be labeled as 'good' or 'bad' in a profession. It is necessary to have the right balance of various emotional competencies that can help one become a star performer. We have also found that although many professions exhibited moderate EQ, it should not be interpreted that high EQ is not required in these professions.

VI. Emotional Intelligence of IAS Officers

The present study had been conducted at University of Delhi, Department of Psychology by Roopsmita Rajkhowa in 2002. The Indian Administrative Service (IAS) is the highest-ranking civil service in India and is the successor to the erstwhile Indian Civil Service of British India. IAS officers hold key positions in government both at the Centre and in the states. After selection, officers are assigned to a state IAS cadre. During the normal course of a career, they are posted at the sub-division and district, and serve in the state secretariats or as head of departments of field offices. Officers may move from positions at the state, under deputation to the Central Government, central public sector undertakings, recognised autonomous organisations, etc. At a senior level, such as special secretary or secretary to the Central Government, the selected officers usually continue to work till they retire at the age of 60. The IAS examination conducted by the Union Public Service Commission (UPSC) is supposed to extend equal opportunities to all. The Indian Administrative Service is a legacy of the British period; the British, who ruled India for almost two centuries, established a system of bureaucracy whose two outstanding features were its 'elitism' and 'loyalty' to its masters. The system dates back to Macaulay's Report of 1854 that demonstrated his profound belief in liberal education. As an all India service, it is under the ultimate control of the Union Government, but is divided into state cadres, each under the immediate control of a state government. Today, the IAS is the core of the country's administrative structure, which shares its tasks with a number of other all India, central and state services.

The typical IAS officer displays a curious crab-like attitude: he dawdles over the simplest of decisions, vacillates when it comes to taking the big initiative, and displays a keen sense of self preservation. At the first sense of danger, which he can sense rather well, he dives into his shell and shirks all responsibility. His dithering is born out of fear that he will be trapped in some departmental enquiry, face suspension or transfer or receive an termination order terminating for taking some action that annoys the people who wield influence. So, there is a heightened sense of insecurity and frustration that paralyses initiative, drive, zeal or enthusiasm. He is unable to go out of his way to clear files that are stuck in the bureaucratic labyrinth because he fears he will be suspected of showing undue favour in exchange for some gratification. If he goes strictly by the rules, he is accused of harassing the public and is labeled a heartless bureaucrat. Hence, the civil servant is often confused about the correct course of action. Emotionally they are not in a position to express themselves due to their high status and position in the government and in society. Most tend to suffer from depression and loneliness at the height of their career, where they cannot share their thoughts, values and perceptions with their seniors or colleagues. He is often forced into a tense standoff with fellow bureaucrats, politicians, businessmen and the judiciary. Despite a well-laid-down policy on transfers and postings of officials, politicians interfere in appointments by transferring their favourite officials to their constituencies or areas of influence, irrespective of whether this is in accordance with the policy. Senior bureaucrats are often shunted out of their positions if they try to resist such interference. Bureaucrats become demoralised and feel humiliated, angry, disgruntled and extremely unhappy. They seem to have no remedy against such situations and silently bear the pain. Often, businessmen and industrialists form a nexus with politicians and put pressure on these officers; sometimes, even MLAs and MPs make unreasonable demands and ill-treat bureaucrats. Bureaucrats often tolerate this, but sometimes there are angry exchanges. The higher judiciary often serves contempt notices on bureaucrats for failing to comply with High Court orders, though the bureaucrats may not be wholly or directly concerned with the subject. This creates unnecessary tension and conflict; and officers have to often tender apologies before the court in accordance with the existing law of the land. Sometimes, the media also joins hands with politicians in order to get petty favours from them. The Press publishes unauthenticated reports against bureaucrats that hurt and demotivate an able officer.

Bureaucrats themselves have axes to grind, resulting in conflicts amongst themselves. There have been innumerous instances of senior bureaucrats maltreating juniors, writing unfavourable assessment reports on the performance of non-complying juniors, being unsympathetic to juniors' genuine problems, expecting too much from young, inexperienced officers, or vying with each other for top positions in the hierarchy. Such conflicts create confusion in administration, slow down the development process, lower the efficiency in delivery of public services and bring a bad image to the entire bureaucracy.

This pioneering research has been carried out using the emotional intelligence test published in the first edition of this book. The researchers were increasingly convinced that negligent amount of work has been done in this area and they undertook this study to get a deeper insight into emotional makeup of Indian Administrative Service (IAS). An attempt has been made in this study to establish the EQ of IAS officers in India. The problem is an open-ended one with no hypothesis made in advance, as it is an exploratory study.

The objectives of the present study were twofold:

1. To make a profile of the various EQ levels of IAS officers, and
2. To compare the emotional intelligence of Group I and Group II (46–60 years) officers and to examine significant differences, if any, between the groups.

The sample consisted of 60 IAS officers belonging to the Assam cadre. The sample was further divided into two groups on the basis of age. Group I consisted of officers in the age group of 30 years to 45 years and Group II, consisting of officers in the age group of 46 to 60 years. In the present study, incidental sampling technique was used. This is part of the non-probability sampling technique, which states that there is no way of estimating the probability that each element has an equal chance of being included in the sample. This technique is characterised by collecting data from the first available individuals of the population.

The tool used for the present study was a structured questionnaire called Emotional Intelligence Test developed by Professor N.K. Chadha (see Chapter 7). The selection of EQ test was guided by the applicability of the measure in the Indian context, high reliability and validity of the instrument and ease in its administration. After selecting the sample, all the respondents were provided with an idea about the purpose of the study. The EQ test was administered after necessary instructions were given to the respondents. Only willing respondents were given the questionnaire, a rapport was established and maintained throughout the period of data collection. Maximum care was taken to see that no item was omitted and respondents were assured that their individual results would be kept confidential.

The findings have been summarised in Table 5.7.

TABLE 5.7: Mean and Standard Deviation (N = 60) on the Variable of Emotional Intelligence

Variable	Mean	Standard Deviation
Emotional intelligence scores	222.75	30.63

Table 5.7 indicates that the sample has a mean of 222.75 with a dispersion of 30.63. This implies that the sample falls in the average to high level of EQ and has homogeneity. In other words, EQ is normally distributed in the sample with a large number of IAS officers falling in the middle category.

TABLE 5.8: Comparison between Group I and Group II IAS Officers

Variable	Group I (30–45 yrs) Mean	SD	Group II (46–60 yrs) Mean	SD	t Value
Emotional intelligence	218.33	28.59	227.16	32.42	0.975

Table 5.8 shows that means for emotional intelligence are 218.33 and 227.16 for Group I and Group II respectively, and the SD scores obtained are 28.59 and 32.42 respectively for both the groups. It can be seen here that the mean for Group II is higher than the mean of Group I, as is the standard deviation score. The t obtained for the Group I and Group II officers has not been found to be significant for the variable of emotional intelligence, i.e., no significant difference between the means was noted on the variable emotional intelligence across ages.

The data obtained has further been presented graphically for better understanding. Table 5.9 shows the profile of the various

TABLE 5.9: EQ Level of IAS Officers

Sr. No.	EQ Level	No. of Officers
1	High	9
2	Average	46
3	Below average	5
	Total	**60**

levels of EQ under which the IAS officers fall (absolute numbers). An individual is allotted to a particular level according to his/her score obtained.

It is evident from Table 5.9 that the majority of officers are in the 'average' category of emotional intelligence, i.e., 46 out of a total number of 60 officers, which is around 77 per cent, while 15 per cent are in the high EQ level and the remaining in the low EQ level. A graphical representation of the same is shown in Figure 5.4.

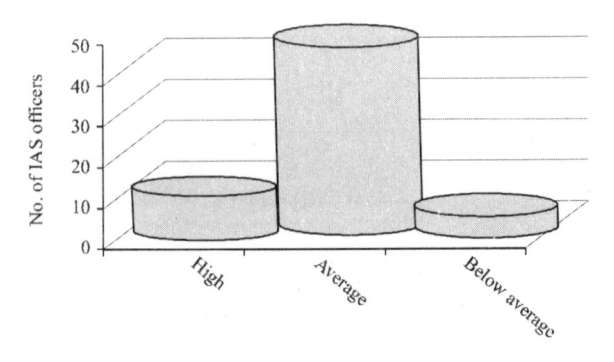

FIGURE 5.4: EQ Level

Interpretation of the results shows that on emotional intelligence, the mean scores for the total sample has been found to be 222.75; this score falls under the percentile rank of P-50, which is average. It is seen that 77 per cent of IAS officers fall in this category. It appears that a moderate level of EQ is sufficient for dealing effectively with their organisational needs and job requirements: acknowledging and understanding the feelings of self and others, and handling stress and conflicting situations. However, 15 per cent of IAS officers have shown high EQ scores, implying thereby that there seems to be a trend among IAS officers to move from moderate to high EQ scores.

For Group I (30–45 years) and Group II (46–60 years), the means for emotional intelligence are 218.33 and 227.16, respectively. It may be observed that Group II is slightly higher on the EQ score as compared to Group I. This indicates development of

EQ with age, although the scores of both groups fall in the average EQ category. The variation in scores, i.e., standard deviation is also found to be higher in Group II than in Group I. This shows that the older group among the IAS officers is higher on EQ than the younger group though the difference is not statistically significant. In other words, it appears that EQ is independent on age. This raises a question: Can EQ increase with age? Maybe one can acquire more knowledge and maturity as one grows older. Age also seems to bring more experience and help in handling the hassles in life.

VII. Emotional Intelligence and Leadership Behaviour

Introduction

B.K. Punia (2005), in the study conducted by him, found that leaders with higher emotional intelligence see changes as opportunities for betterment, and they cherish not stability but ongoing development of individual workers and of the organisation itself. This entire phenomenon paradigm shift delves into the concept of emotional intelligence and leadership behaviour. The basic contention of this research is to develop a generalist view about the impact of emotional intelligence on leadership behaviour of Indian corporate executives. The paper unfolds the existing leadership frame vis-à-vis emotional intelligence level of Indian executives, drawn with help of standard scales on the subjects. The paper concludes with certain important guidelines for enhancing leadership effectiveness through emotional intelligence specifically tailored to Indian industrial environment.

In Indian business, CEOs are often heard saying 'business done by brain and not by heart'. They view that people with low emotional intelligence lead to low productivity and poor management. Indian professional approach at large could be felt to be very traditional, i.e., non-emotional approach devoid of personal relations. Many fatal flaws are related to classical emotional failures, such as poor working relations, authoritarianism or excessive ambition and conflict with top management. It is healthy for mind, body, heart and spirit to experience feelings as and when they arise. Leaders who are attuned to their own feelings and the feelings of others can use their understanding to enhance the organisation's effectiveness.

Scope and Methodology

The study at hand has been conducted to examine the leadership frame of Indian executives, their level of emotional intelligence, and also to ascertain the impact of emotional intelligence on leadership orientation and behaviour of the executives. The study also aims at suggesting guidelines for enhancing leadership effectiveness through emotional intelligence. Though study has been conducted in the Indian subcontinent yet its findings can be equally useful for rest of the Asian countries due to similarities in the work cultures. In the present study an exploratory-cum-descriptive research design has been followed to reach at the above-mentioned objectives. Data has been collected from 250 executives by applying convenience-cum-purposive sampling. Though data has been collected from the executives working in different organisations of the National Capital Region, Delhi, yet due care has been taken to pick up the respondents from diverse geographical regions and religions to make the sample representative. The data has been collected with the help of three scales/inventories developed by three distinct authorities in their respective fields. The first scale on Leadership Orientation helps in studying the four-leadership frames, i.e., structural, human resource, political and symbolic frames of a learning organisation. This scale consists of six questions with four options of each and the respondents were asked to rank them from four to one to ascertain their leadership frame. Lawrence Otis Graham has developed the second research instrument on Leadership Development that aims at knowing the 'passive bias' of a leader. This instrument consists of 12 statements to be answered in yes or no, and gives a leader's behaviour in his surroundings and its impact on decision-making, as a leader should definitely consider ways to become more diversity aware and culturally sensitive. The third instrument, an Emotional Intelligence Test, has been developed by N.K. Chadha, a psychologist at University of Delhi. This test consists of 15 different situations with five options of each to measure the level of emotional intelligence in a leader. The data collected with the above mentioned there research instruments has been duly analysed, interpreted and correlated to reach at the objectives of the study.

Results and Discussion

The data collected with the help of research instruments has been analysed and interpreted on the basis of different demographic factors like age, sex and marital status. As the organisations of the day are operating in the global world, hence it calls for dealing with diversity on a broader stage than ever before. Dimensions of diversity are both primary such as gender, age and secondary such as marital status, religion etc. There are several reasons for organisations for recognising the need to value and support the prevailing cultural diversity. This phenomenon of diversity has made the task of the present day business leaders much challenging. Only those leaders with higher amount of emotional stability are expected to be more effective and gain competitive advantage. The ensuing discussion deals with unfolding the existing leadership frames, passive bias towards diversity and emotional intelligence level of Indian executives on the basis of three variables—age, gender and marital status to ascertain the leadership styles in relation to emotional intelligence in learning organisations.

Impact of Age on Emotional Intelligence and Leadership Behaviour

Age-wise respondents were categorised in four age groups, i.e., executives with less than 25 years, 26–35 years, 36–45 and above 45 years of age. The results on the leadership frames reveal that personnel below 25 years of age and those in the age group of 26–35 are of multiple type leadership frames, while those in age groups of more than 35 years are of humanistic frame. This connotes that the young generation of executives have long-range vision and they recognise and support a diverse organisational community. It also signifies that lower age group executives are more willing to work in global world and trap opportunities from various cultures by capturing unique characteristics of others. However the personnel above 35 years of age have been found less prone to multiple orientations as their experience has turned them to be humanistic and ensnare the opportunities in the same culture instead of diversified one. The results further illustrate the level of passive bias of executives in relation to their age. It can be gauged that personnel above 45 years of age have high passive bias, while a absolute passive bias is totally absent from any of the age groups. Though a medium level of bias has been recorded significantly in every age group, yet it is highest in the executives who are less than 25 years of age. Hence it can be concluded that the degree of passive bias increases with age, which in turn indicates that the executives with growing age resist changes, and like to work in their own manner. The phenomenon of resistance to change increases bias, which is neither appropriate nor desirable for the individual, organisation and the society at large. The results demonstrate the emotional intelligence level of the executives in relation to their age reveals a parabolic trend. It means that a person's emotional intelligence level first increases with the age, reach at a peak and than start decreasing. In the age group of below 25 years about 50 per cent respondents have an average level of emotional intelligence; those in the age groups of 26–35 years and 36–45 years have recorded high level of emotional intelligence to the tune of 39 per cent and 54 per cent respectively. 80 per cent of personnel above 45 years of age have shown an average level of emotional intelligence. Thus the respondents above 25 years but less than 45 years of age have witnessed comparatively more emotional stability.

The analysis above concludes that the person's leadership style changes with age. As and when a person is less willing to adapt to changes and bring diversity, it will lead to a bias. The reason behind this lies in the fact that with growing age though a person's emotional stability increases, but after peak it starts declining thereby creating proportionate relationship between emotional intelligence and leadership behaviour of the executives.

Impact of Marital Status on Emotional Intelligence and Leadership Behaviour

Generally, it is believed that a person's life gets a sea change after marriage due to additional responsibilities, changes in the priorities, interchange of culture etc. This occurrence of change is bound to affect the performance of the person at the work place as well and the industry executives who are already burdened with the office work. Therefore, to what extent the marital status affect the emotional stability, leadership frame and the bias of executives at work place is very relevant and timely in this milieu. The findings reveal that unmarried executives generally opt for multiple frames followed by structural frame of leadership. Married executives give equal preference to multiple and humanistic frame of leadership. It is also worth noting a fact that unmarried executives did not register their option for humanistic and symbolic frame at all. This difference in the leadership frames perhaps may be due to other factors and additional responsibilities and not because of marriage. Though the degree of biases is affected least according to martial status yet the married executives are comparatively biased as compared to unmarried executives. Though emotional intelligence does not seem to be dependent on the marital status of a person yet it gives some interesting findings on the subject. The level of emotional intelligence in both the categories, i.e., married and unmarried executives has been found to be high or average, however unmarried executives have registered higher amount of emotional stability. Comparatively lower emotional intelligence in the married executives seems to be an outcome of overwork and additional and diverse type of responsibilities. The analysis of above shows that there is not significant correlation between martial status, emotional intelligence and leadership behaviour. Whatever little variations have been observed seem to be an outcome of other factors and not that of marriage.

Impact of Gender on Emotional Intelligence and Leadership Behaviour

Men and women are two equal partners of the society, and even Indian constitution does not permit to discriminate on the basis of sex. However Indian women generally have to face discrimination due to her being female. Though this tendency is disappearing with advancement of the society yet it has not fully liberated from it. The change in the attitude of the society has also led the corporate world to change its outlook and attitude towards women executives. Many research studies have been conducted and the growing organisations' philosophy towards gender equality has come in the form that today women are expected to 'look like lady and act like man'. Moreover the organisations of the day are now emphasising on the women leadership due to specific advantages of the same and we find hardly any organisation/department where women are not leading. May be it is service sector, manufacturing sector or any other administrative assignment women have marked their presence in bold. In spite of this all certain misgivings with regard to leadership styles of women executives are still present in the Indian minds. So whatever variations emerge on emotional intelligence and leadership behaviour executives on the basis of gender is the subject of discussion for this section.

The study clearly brings out the leadership frames as adopted by the executives. It can be envisaged that men executives generally go for multiple frame of leadership in contrast to female executives who are more oriented towards structural and humanistic frame. This supports the fact that male executives are accepted more as the marketing, production personnel and are developed as such, while women executives are more acceptable in human resource management, financial management (office job) departments due to her leadership frame and orientation of being structural or humanistic. The wide difference on the basis of sex has made the Indian women to believe that the marketing field is not her first cup of tea and that is why the number of women executives in this field are comparatively less but those who have established themselves herein are very successful. The findings also portray the level of passive biases in both the genders and it may be observed that male executives are more prone to bias as compared to the female executives. Female executives being more humanistic and tolerant have been found less biased in decision-making. In the Indian culture it is the general saying that female is another name of sacrifice and patience, which in turn speaks about her emotional stability. The gender wise level of emotional intelligence shows that women are more emotionally stable due to their high level of emotional intelligence. EQ of majority female executives has been found high and average; where as the male counterparts are low in the EQ level which leads us to conclude that women are more capable of handling the people and recognising their needs as compared to men. Hence it can be concluded from the above discussion that women executives go for humanistic or structural frame of leadership in contrast to male executives who go for larger amount of multiple frame. Male executives' decisions are generally more biased as compared to female executives and women executives have been found more emotionally stable making them effective leaders.

Conclusion

The opening up of the Indian economy through liberalisation, privatisation, globalisation and natural thrust towards information technology had made the task of Indian managers more demanding. The challenges get multiplied when the industry executives have to work in diversified work cultures. The workforce diversity has not only affected the emotional stability of the executives but has also come on the way of leadership behaviour and effectiveness. In the present study it is found that a person's leadership style changes with age. As and when a person is less willing to adapt to changes and bring diversity, it will lead to a bias. The reason behind this lies in the fact with growing age though a person's emotional stability increases, but after peak it start declining thereby creating proportionate relationship between emotional intelligence and leadership behaviour of the executives. Marriage does not come much on the way of a leader in terms of his behaviour, and emotional stability. Women executives have been found with humanistic or structural frame of leadership. Male executives' decisions are more biased as compared to female executives but women executives have been found more emotionally intelligent. In nutshell tomorrow is the day of those industry executives who are more emotionally stable and show leadership effectiveness even in diverse circumstances irrespective of their age, marital status or gender.

The study shows the linkage between emotional intelligence of leader and the performance indicates a positive correlation. When a leader exhibits competencies like initiative, nurturing attitude, team building, self-confidence, achievement motivation, and empathy etc, the performance is bound to be more effective. The results of the study can be translated into specific suggestion to enhance leadership effectiveness and that through emotional intelligence. A leader's passion for work reasons less for money or power and his ability to pursue goals vigorously and persistently are more important. Instead of securing short-term gains, achievement for the sake of achievement should be the goal of every manager and which in turn need high level of achievement motivation in the leader to help him in leading from the front. Every leader should be aware that his job is as much about getting people to work together as a team, as it is about motivating individual member of the team. Thus, the leader's aim should be to build a team, which is cohesive, self-supporting and must know where it is going. In order to develop a team spirit, high morale and induce a feeling of shared responsibility for achievement, the leader must foster an environment of mutual trust and confidence and create a feeling of interdependence among the team members.

VIII. Relation between EQ and IQ among Adolescents

Lakshmi Sitaram (2005) defines the term adolescence as to be the period of transition from dependence to self-dependence. Adolescence is generally considered to include the years from the onset of puberty, or approximately age 11, through age 19 years. The overall growth and development leads adolescents to experience anxieties and uncertainties, which adds to the adjustment problems of the youth. It has been found that the most common causes of all the problems among adolescents are mental illness, poor ability in resolving conflicts and handling emotions. Understanding the characteristics, needs, interests, problems and growth potential of maturing adolescents is necessary to help them experience a gradual and relatively peaceful development from early childhood to adulthood. In some cases, excellent emotional control, social adaptability and intelligent behaviour are evident, while in others little evidence of maturity in these developmental aspects is seen. In fact, the term intelligent behaviour is being substituted for intelligence, to stress the functional implication of its meaning. Intelligence involves not just a single ability; its multiple abilities, categorised as cognitive and non-cognitive intelligences, assess a person's performance in more than one domain. The children who are better able to cope with stress, get along with others and enjoy their lives become less impulsive and more successful problem solvers and adapters.

Adjustment in adolescents is defined as a continuous process of maintaining harmony among the attributes of self and the environmental conditions that surround them. Adjustment is just an ability to select appropriate and effective measures to meet the demands of the environment while maintaining a healthy attitude towards the circumstances. During adolescence, when the body changes from that of a growing child to that of an adult, this change needs adjustment in both physical and psychological aspects.

Among the innumerable variables that may influence adjustment, birth order and demographic factors are the most influencing ones. Birth order is the sequence of birth of children in a given family. Other demographic factors like age, gender, type of family, socio economic status, number of siblings must also be considered. Adolescents who are normally known to be emotionally maladjusted can be identified through this study and studied in relation to their social environment.

The objective of the present study is to understand intelligence, emotional intelligence and adjustment and also to find the relationships between intelligence, emotional intelligence and adjustment among adolescents. The sample included a population comprising male and female adolescents in the age range of 15–16 years. A majority of them belonged to nuclear families and nearly 41 per cent of the families had two children, while 48 per cent of the families belonged to a mid-socio-economic background.

The significant findings of the empirical research are summarised as under:

- **Overall assessment of adolescents** The results reveal that most of the adolescents fall under the average category on intelligence, emotional intelligence and on adjustment too. On intelligence, 41 per cent of adolescents fall under average category while on emotional intelligence, 50 per cent were found to have average emotional intelligence. On adjustment, again 50 per cent males were found to have average adjustment while in females 45 per cent of them had average adjustment.
- **Factors affecting intelligence** Except for gender, all other factors like age group, birth order, type of family and socio economic statuses was found to have influenced the performance of adolescents on intelligence.
- **Factors affecting emotional intelligence** The patterns of emotional intelligence levels did not vary much with the influence of gender, age, birth order and type of family. The only factor, which was found have affected the performance on emotional intelligence was socio economic statuses of adolescents.
- **Factors affecting adjustment and its dimensions** According to the result, the factors that influenced overall adjustment were age, type of family, birth order and socio economic status.
- **Correlation among intelligence, emotional intelligence and adjustment** Correlation between *emotional intelligence and intelligence* reveal that there is a positive correlation between

the both but the correlation per cent was just 19 per cent, which is a mild correlation percentage. *Emotional intelligence* was also found to have positively correlated with *adjustment*. Higher the individual's ability to be aware of his own and others emotions, higher will be the ability to maintain a harmonious relationship between himself and environment. It was also found that *Intelligence* had positive correlation with *adjustment*.

- **Interaction of intelligence, emotional intelligence and adjustment as dependent variables** Regression analysis between the variables, factors and their interactions revealed the following: Adjustment, intelligence, socioeconomic status and an interaction of these variables can be used to predict emotional intelligence. Similarly, it was found that adjustment, emotional intelligence, socioeconomic status and an interaction of these variables can be used to predict intelligence in adolescents. The analysis also revealed that Emotional intelligence and number of siblings can be used to predict adjustment in adolescents.

The study concludes that a positive relation was observed between emotional intelligence, intelligence and also with adjustment. Though the relationship among these are not very strong, it can be stated individuals who can adjust themselves better and who have good intelligence quotient, will be in a better position to cope with stress, get along with others, and enjoy their lives. They are usually found to be less impulsive and more successful problem solvers and adapters. Development of these facets of emotional and personal aspects can significantly help optimise academic potential, interpersonal relationships, and ultimately, life success.

IX. EQ AND MANAGERIAL EFFECTIVENESS: AN INTERNATIONAL STUDY

Objectives

Dalip Singh (2005) explored the nature of management practices in Indian organisations and those that prevail in organisations managed through Japanese, American and European managerial systems. Emotional intelligence and managerial effectiveness have been considered as dependent or consequent variables for the purpose of the study to establish their relationship with the different management styles. In addition, an attempt has been made to arrive at an operational definition of emotional intelligence in the Indian context. Further, this study also looks into gender and positional issues dealing with job-related activities. The interface of managerial effectiveness and emotional intelligence with demographic variables is also subject matter of the study.

Emotional intelligence, and its relevance for organisations, is of utmost importance to modern day managers. Organisations do not deal with materials alone, they also deal with people. The emotional intelligence of an organisation can be judged from the way it deals with issues of leadership, interpersonal relations, communication and relations with other organisations. How do managers counter stressful and conflicting situations? How do they handle frustrations? The answers to some of these questions could reflect the emotional intelligence of a manager.

Managerial effectiveness is a crucial element of an organisation. An organisation's functions and behaviour are influenced by the degree of its managerial effectiveness. If a manager is able to recognise his own strengths and weaknesses and also that of his subordinates, understands the requirements of his job well, uses his own strengths and overcomes weaknesses through continuous learning on the job, he/she may be considered as effective and at the same time successful in motivating the subordinates and achieving the goals of the organisation.

Organisations Studied

Four organisations, with Indian, Japanese, American and European management and operating in India for the last two years, were taken into consideration for the present study. The total sample size was 204, comprising 83 middle-level managers and 121 senior-level managers. Also, the sample consisted of 149 males and 55 females. Only those managers who were at least graduates, with more than five years of experience, aged 26 years or more, and earning more than Rs 20,000 per month were selected randomly for the data collection.

Method of Data Collection

The questionnaire method was used for the purposes of data collection. The Emotional Intelligence Test designed by Chadha (2002), the Managerial Effectiveness Test designed by Kaur (1998) and Information schedule were used. All required precautions were kept in mind while collecting the data. Statistical analysis was done to interpret the results, and which included descriptive analysis, inferential analysis, correlational analysis, content analysis and graphical representation.

Conclusions

The main conclusions of the present study are enumerated below:

1. The Correlational analysis has revealed that there is positive relationship between emotional intelligence and managerial effectiveness of managers. For instance, the managers high on emotional intelligence would generally be high on managerial effectiveness also and vice-versa. *Emotional intelligence* has been recognised as a key determinant to managerial success in today's high stress environment both in life and as work. The available research conducted on the subject shows that people with high emotional intelligence are happier, healthier and more effective on the job. This is because they have an awareness of their feelings and are able to strike a balance between reason and emotions that makes them good leaders and team players. *Managerial Effectiveness* on the other hand is defined as achieving the organisational goals and objectives effectively. From the results of the present findings, it may be concluded that a high and positive relationship exists between emotional intelligence and managerial effectiveness.

2. Another significant conclusion of the present study is that emotional intelligence and experience are found to be positively and significantly related to each other. These findings support the view that experienced managers are more emotionally intelligent than the less experienced ones. Experience may be defined as having more years of service in terms of years, maturity gained over a period of time and during training activities. The present research concludes that as a manager gains more experience and maturity by spending longer periods on a particular job, he/she exhibits higher emotional intelligence.
3. The study also concluded that male and female managers are positively and significantly different on the variable emotional intelligence. The mean scores indicate that female are higher on emotional intelligence as compared to males. The Consortium for Research in Emotional Intelligence in Organisations (2005) has also reported that men and women, as groups, tend to have a shared gender-specific profile of strong and weak points. An analysis of emotional intelligence in thousands of men and women reveal that women were more aware of their emotions, showed more empathy and were adept interpersonally. Men on the other hand were more self-confident and optimistic, adapted more easily and handled stress better.
4. The results obtained were further subjected to comparison among the Indian, Japanese, American and European organisations. The conclusions arrived at are as follows:

- Comparison of managers of **American and European** organisations showed that American managers are high on the variables qualification, level and income, while European managers are high on experience, managerial effectiveness and emotional quotient.
- While comparing managers of **American and Japanese** organisations, it has been observed that American managers are high on qualification, experience, level, managerial effectiveness and emotional quotient. Japanese

managers are high on only one variable as compared to their American counterparts, that is, income.
- Managers of **American and Indian** organisations showed different competencies: American managers are high on qualification, age, income and managerial effectiveness, while perusal of mean scores of their Indian counterparts shows that they are high on experience and emotional quotient.
- Comparison of managers of **European and Japanese** organisations revealed that European managers are high on five variables: qualification, experience, age, managerial effectiveness and emotional quotient. In contrast, Japanese managers are found to be high on only one variable—income.
- While comparing managers of **European and Indian** organisations, it has been observed that European managers are high on qualification, experience, managerial effectiveness and emotional quotient, while Indian managers are high on age and income.
- Managers of **Japanese and Indian** organisations showed different competencies when compared with each other. While Japanese managers are high on the variables qualification and income, Indian managers scored high on experience, age, managerial effectiveness and emotional quotient.

5. The conclusions drawn from the study of the four organisations are now discussed from the perspective of the variables *emotional intelligence*, *managerial effectiveness*, *qualification*, *age*, *experience* and *income*.

EMOTIONAL INTELLIGENCE

The study has revealed that European managers lead in emotional intelligence as compared to the rest of the sample, followed by Indians, Americans and Japanese, in that order. These conclusions may be seen in Figure 5.5.

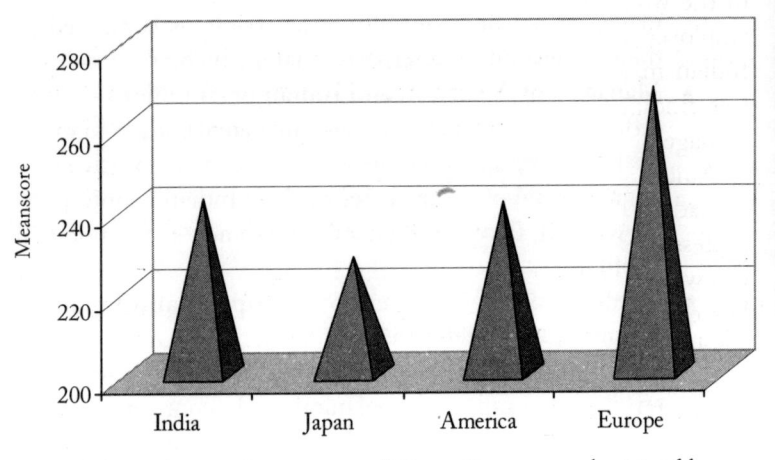

FIGURE 5.5: Comparison of Four Groups on the Variable 'Emotional Intelligence'

It may be concluded that a high score on emotional intelligence by European managers shows that they are emotionally intelligent as compared to others. Although, a European managerial model has not yet been developed, the synthesis of the business cultures of important countries of this region—England, Germany, Italy, France and Sweden—prove that European managers handle their personal and professional life intelligently. For instance, they have a higher degree of risk avoidance and are rather unwilling to take a risk and pursue an uncertain venture. The most successful people in life are considered to be the ones who have learned to manage their emotional reactions, to neutralise or transform negative emotions and processes and gain new richness of experience. Spencer (1997) analysed more than 300 top-level executives from 15 global companies and found that characteristics like achievement drive and leadership emotional competencies distinguished 'star performers' from the average.

The results also show that Indian managers are high on emotional intelligence, coming just after the Europeans. This significant finding is clearly reflective of Indian management culture and business environment. Indian firms reflect an emotional environment with elements of familial bonding being carried over to the workplace, as seen in relationships between employer and employee (Chadha 2005). This explanation leaves no doubt that Indian managers are indeed high on emotional intelligence and this finding is perfectly in tune with the philosophy of Indian management systems.

American managers are also high on emotional intelligence and adopt emotionally intelligent behaviour in their personal and professional life. This phenomenon may be explained by the American way of living. People in the West grow up with comparatively less emotional security due to factors such as high divorce rates, single parent families, and so on. As they grow up, they find a sense of stability in their seemingly unstable and insecure atmosphere. Thus, when they start working and find a management culture that is contractual in nature, with a hire-and-fire style, they are not disturbed. In fact, such a situation motivates them to work harder. The net outcome of such management practice is that the Americans have learned to manage their emotions intelligently early in life. This also helps them in their professional life by making them adept at tackling the turbulent situations on the job: retrenchments, contractual agreements and hire-and-fire management systems, stress, frustration, burnout, anxiety and interpersonal conflicts. It may be concluded that the American system of management teaches managers to manage their emotions intelligently.

Although Japanese managers are lower on EQ as compared to European, Indian and American managers, they are in the category of moderate emotional intelligence. The Japanese believe in lifelong employment, where workers spent their entire working life with a single enterprise, which in turn provides employees a feeling of security and belongingness. The Japanese reflect group behaviour where every one helps the other for a common cause. They have a culture of sharing, where even enemies help each other in order to survive, and this is an important indicator of emotional intelligence. This also explains why the Japanese, in general, feel that they are part of a larger community where what they do is important to everyone. This culture enables Japanese managements to get considerable involvement from workers.

Their emotional bonding is reflected in simple gestures such as the top brass and ordinary staff wearing the same uniform, eating in the same canteen and using the same parking lot. Hence, the conclusion that the Japanese have a moderate level of emotional intelligence is in tune with their management model.

MANAGERIAL EFFECTIVENESS

The comparison of managers of the four organisations reveals that the European managers have highest managerial effectiveness, followed by the Americans, Indians and Japanese in that order. The comparisons are shown given in Figure 5.6.

European managers are high on managerial effectiveness which is in harmony with European management model, and characterised by its strength in engineering, technical training and craft. Their emphasis is on managing the organisation effectively by way of acquiring more and more knowledge and skills. Such a professional approach is crucial for being an effective manager. Hence, it is no surprise that European organisations working in India are high on managerial effectiveness.

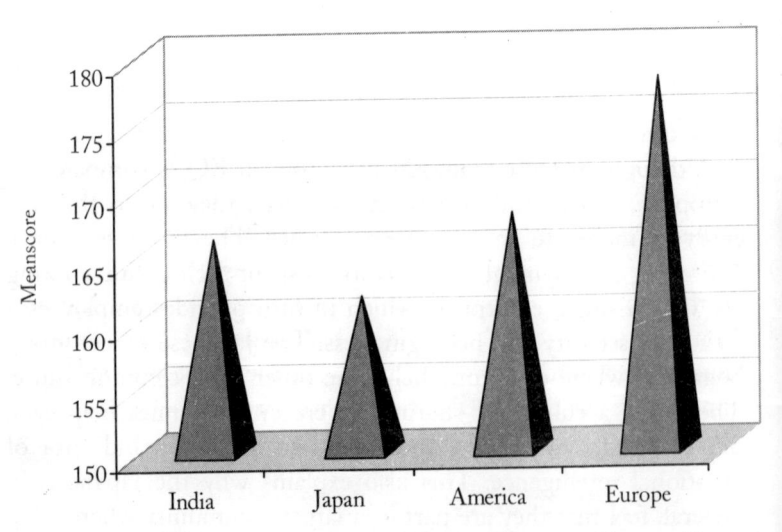

FIGURE 5.6: Comparison of Four Groups on the Variable 'Managerial Effectiveness'

The Americans also believe in three well-established dimensions of management—technical, conceptual and human—which are fully reflected in the American management culture. They have also tuned themselves to develop and upgrade their managerial skills over a period of time. They see competition as one of the most productive ways of distributing awards. All these managerial components make American managers more effective than others, as found in the present study.

We find that on managerial effectiveness, Indians rank after Europeans and Americans. This is reflective of the fact that Indian management ethos are largely borrowed from American or European management systems. Indian business is becoming 'professional' due to global competitiveness. The economy is opening up and restrictions on the industry and business have largely been removed. The private sector is also opening up and sharing the profits with social responsibility. The country has made remarkable progress in information technology, telecommunication, agriculture, technical education, medical science and many other areas. It may therefore be concluded that the modern day business knowledge has resulted in managerial effectiveness of Indian managers.

Japanese managers have scored lowest on the variable managerial effectiveness. Although the Japanese management system is a well-managed, coordinated style of management, its employees working in India are found to be low on managerial effectiveness. This could be because Japanese organisations have a drawback in terms of inefficient monitoring of and lack of control over their top management. Another reason could be the practice of 'rotation' in the Japanese system where managerial staff is moved around from job to job over the years. The rotation is fairly frequent, usually every two or three years, giving the employees very little time to learn the job well. These factors seem to have resulted in them having low scores on managerial effectiveness.

QUALIFICATION

The results obtained indicate that American managers have higher qualifications as compared to the rest of the group. Further, the Japanese and Europeans are next in the order, and Indian managers being least qualified.

These findings are significant in that they show that the American business and management culture motivates a manager to acquire more and more academic and professional qualifications in order to move up in the hierarchy. The same appears to be true in the case of Japan and Europe where also technical, professional or on-the-job qualifications are considered important. However, the Indian system of management does not appear to support this view as Indian managers are seen to be the least qualified. This could be due to the fact that the importance of 'Professional Management' is not yet considered very important in India.

EXPERIENCE

The findings also reveal that the European managers more years of experience. Indians and Americans follow them in that order, and the Japanese have the least work experience.

It may be noticed that all four groups have moderate to high work experience. This shows that they all value experience of a manager to achieve organisational goals. These findings are in tune with the different management cultures prevalent in these countries. For instance, the European management system is considered to be professional in nature. In case of India, since professional management has not yet picked up, there is a tendency to depend on the experience of managers and workers. As far as American management system is concerned, they still believe that managerial skills cannot be completely taught and being able to deal effectively with other persons is either an inborn skill or can only be developed and upgraded over a period of time. Though the Japanese managers have scored low as compared to the rest of the group, they value lifetime employment and link seniority with wages and promotion.

AGE

While comparing the four groups on the variable age, it has been found that American managers are of the higher age, followed by the Indians, Europeans and Japanese, in that order.

This shows that the American management system has more senior managers in the higher age groups. In the case of India, a lower age level indicates that young managers can also join and occupy managerial positions. The same is true of European and Japanese management systems that encourage younger managers to participate in the decision-making process. This may also indicate the beginning of professional management practices in India.

INCOME

The comparison of the four groups on the variable income has shown interesting results. For instance, Japanese managers have the highest income level, followed by Americans. The Indian managers have higher incomes as compared to their European counterparts but lower than that of the Japanese and Americans. Significantly enough, though, Europeans have the lowest incomes.

These findings indicate that the Japanese and American organisations are giving higher wages to their Indian employees to maintain the best international standards. Interestingly, Indian organisations are also paying their employees well mainly due to global competition and demand on quality. The European organisations are found to be paying lower wages to its employees in India. This may be because of acute unemployment coupled with the availability of a sufficient number of professionally qualified managers who are willing to work for lower wages, especially in foreign organisations. Such an offer gives Indian managers international exposure, competitive experience and a sense of self-esteem while working with a foreign employer.

X. EQ AND WELL-BEING OF ADOLESCENTS

Meena Sehgal (1999) proposes that health professionals have become increasingly concerned with physiological well-being and ways to promote it, rather than focus on negative dimensions like anxiety, depression and insecurity. Some of the most common indicators of positive well-being are happiness, optimism and life satisfaction. Self-esteem has been defined as the personal evaluation of one's worth; happiness as the balance between positive and negative effects; life satisfaction as a 'global evaluation by the person of his or her life'; and optimism as the 'general tendency to expect a favourable outcome in one's life'. Presumably, people who believe that their actions will lead to favourable outcomes will persist in those actions. If there are individual differences in the tendency to expect success, optimists would achieve more and have more good things happen to them. For researchers who emphasise on social fabric, the theory of life satisfaction as the key indictor of well-being has gained significance. Life satisfaction seems to complement happiness. Some other researchers have theorised about Psychological Well-Being. A multidimensional model of Well-Being which includes dimensions of Self Acceptance, Positive Relations with others, Sense of Autonomy Environmental Mastery.

Purpose in Life and Personal Growth is being termed as most effective. In late 1995 and early 1996, another concept, Emotional IQ (Emotional Intelligence) or EQ, was identified as the key to success, well-being and successful relationship. Studies from hundreds of companies, mostly multinational, has identified the following qualities of EQ which make people 'the best from the rest' and highly successful, an important aspect of well-being. Some of the major qualities that make up emotional intelligence are: (*a*) Self awareness, (*b*) Mood management, or control over emotions, (*c*) Self motivation or positive motivation which is the marshalling of feelings of enthusiasm, zeal and confidence, (*d*) Impulse control i.e., the essence of emotional self-regulation and the ability to delay impulse in the service of a goal, and (*e*) People Skills or the capacity to know how others feel and develop good interpersonal skills.

It has been opined that it is not Intelligence (Intelligent Quotient) alone, but EQ (Emotional Quotient) as well, that contributes to success, happiness, life satisfaction and the feeling of well-being.

The present study was an exploratory attempt to investigate the relationship between EQ, intelligence, psychological well-being and the Eysenckian Personality dimensions.

Sample

The sample consisted of 150 adolescents—75 girls and 75 boys—between 15 and 17 years of age, selected randomly from Model Schools in Chandigarh.

Tests & Tools

1. Eysenck Personality Questionnaire (Eysenck & Eysenck 1975).
2. Psychological Well-Being (Verma & Verma 1989).
3. Cattell's Culture Fair Intelligence Test (1971).
4. EQ inventory, constructed based on Goleman's concept of EQ.

Results and Discussion

Means, standard deviations (SD) and *t*-ratios were calculated separately for girls and boys. As none of the *t*-ratios emerged as significant, the sample was pooled and treated as one large group (N = 150) of adolescents. Inter-correlations were calculated among various measures and the results are presented in Table 5.10.

TABLE 5.10: Means, SDs and Intercorrelations (N=150)

	M	SD	Correlations of EQ with	
1. Emotional Quotient	24.34	2.84	1. Psychoticism	–.07
2. Psychoticism	6.73	3.14	2. Extraversion	.11
3. Extraversion	13.72	3.9	3. Neuroticism	.02
4. Neuroticism	9.83	4.53	4. Lie Score	.08
5. Lie Score	8.62	3.94	5. Intelligence	.20
6. Intelligence	29.53	6.35	6. Psychological Well-Being	.24**
7. Psychological Well-Being	18.13	3.31		

*Significant at .05 level, **Significant at .01 level.

As can be seen in Table 5.10, EQ and IQ dimensions show a moderate significant positive correlation; Psychological Well-Being also showed high significant positive correlation with EQ. However, none of the Eysenckian personality dimensions were related to EQ. Most earlier researches have linked personality with emotional experiences. Theoretically, one would have expected a positive correlation between Extraversion and EQ and negative correlations between Neuroticism, Psychoticism and EQ. However, an Israeli psychologist, Reuven Bar-On, who made the first commercially available test to measure EQ, defined emotional intelligence as 'capabilities, competencies and skills that influence one's ability to succeed in coping with environmental demands and pressures which directly affect one's overall Psychological Well-Being'. Bar-On 1997 reported low insignificant correlations between the EQ dimensions of his test and Eysenckian dimensions of Personality. Perhaps, Personality and Well-Being represent conceptually distinct constructs. Personality traits are stable patterns of behaviour, whereas Well-Being is a desirable psychological state that may change in response to life's achievements. As proposed by Goleman and Reuven Bar-On, EQ was related positively with Psychological Well-Being among adolescents in the present study. To conclude, one may safely propose that the concept of EQ can go a long way in being used as an index of Well-Being and mental health, and it can be advocated that this dimension potentially makes for successful, and psychologically and mentally healthy, individuals.

XI. THE SOFT ART OF BEING A TOUGH LEADER

Parmananda Chabungban (2005) proposes that by developing Emotional Intelligence one can build a bridge between stress and better performance. In leadership and managing, the soft skills that a person needs are as important as some of the other skill sets that he/she brings on board. Stress management, one of the dimensions of human resource management, involves several soft skills, while the concept of Emotional Intelligence (EQ) is logically qualified to be called the hub of a larger set of soft skills.

Stress is not always bad, but it is a much-quoted ailment at work. The effects of stress are costly to both the organisation and the employee if left unattended within a given timeframe. Indeed, stress at the workplace is actually a barometer of the health of an organisation. The problem is that havoc is wreaked below the surface and mild symptoms of stress are often hidden. The symptoms of stress are typically grouped under three categories: mental (anxiety, anger, mood swings, absence of humour), physical (headache, neck ache, sweating, indigestion, weight gain or loss), and behavioural (acting on impulse, stuttering, drug dependency, changing jobs). When its severity increases and proper intervention not done at the right time, the individual may 'hit the wall' or even attempt suicide. In the workplace, this results in high absenteeism, high rate of accidents, reduced effectiveness, high attrition and other corporate expenses.

EQ is the ability of person to control impulses and persist in the face of frustration and obstacles, prevent negative emotions from swamping the ability to think, feel motivated and confident and to accurately perceive emotions, to empathise and get along well with others. It has two spectrums: intra-personal skills and inter-personal skills. They are the causal factors of distress, and at the same time for panacea.

Today it is widely believed that EQ, rather than IQ, is the true measure of human intelligence. Many studies indicate that school grades and IQ are weak predictors of success in life. It is also known now that IQ cannot be developed, whereas EQ can be developed throughout one's life span. In the workplace, IQ can help you get hired, but it is your EQ that gets you promotion and recognition. Emotional skills help push towards better performance. It is therefore important to understand the true economic value of EQ.

Emotional intelligence and performance are correlated. The human body has a self-controlled feedback system that utilises its resources for homoeostasis—the tendency of the human body to maintain internal equilibrium. Distress denotes a break in normal homoeostatic functioning in the event of a mismatch between individual capability and 'demands'. People usually assume that it is important to reduce stress to prevent burnout (an extreme form of stress). But 'rustout', the opposite of burnout, is no less important. If an employee's capacity is more than what his work demands, he may experience rustout; if his capacity is not meeting the demand, he may enjoy peak performance; and if his actual capacity is not meeting the demand, then burnout is a possible results. In all three conditions, employees need self-regulation to increase stress respectively to keep it at the optimum. And, this is where the performance of EQ is hailed.

Every individual has a 'rational self'; but when exposed to stressor(s), it is often pushed aside by stress-building thoughts and disrupts performance. We can learn to avoid stress-building thoughts and replace them with 'stress-busting' thoughts. Consider these two situations:

1. Stress-builder: 'My boss did not respond to my "good morning". He is displeased with my work. I will get a bad appraisal.'
2. Stress-buster: 'My boss may be in bad mood, but I should not be in judgement of this. Unless I get a negative feedback, I believe he is happy with me.'

The EQ framework incorporates dimensions like self-awareness, flexibility, tolerance, optimism, empathy and social skills (the ability to get along with others, to work well in teams, to handle conflicts) that directly or indirectly contribute to stress management. It is also true that EI influences performance. There are interesting findings by Haygroup that high-EI executive teams out-perform business targets by 15–20 per cent, and high EI organisations have greater agility, resilience and focus. A 40-year longitudinal study on 450 boys at Sommerville showed that IQ has a bearing on performance at work. However, childhood abilities to handle frustration, control emotions and get along with people have direct links with work performance. Another study came up with the finding that store managers who are able to manage their own stress and stay unaffected have the most profitable stores, and that outstanding flight attendants respond calmly to disgruntled passengers. Similarly, among counsellors, superior performers tend to respond calmly to angry attacks by clients. Individuals who scored higher in the ability to perceive, understand and appraise other's emotions were better able to respond flexibly to changes in their social environments and build supportive social networks. A study carried out in UK's police service gives a lucid picture about the positive impact of EQ in successfully coping with stressful encounters. Another study on 62 CEOs and their top management teams found that more positive the emotions of people in management teams, the better are the company's business results (4–6 per cent higher market-adjusted earnings per share) than companies with members of diverse emotional outlooks.

Managers who attended a training programme on understanding emotional responses and relating them to their thoughts and behaviour showed significant increase in their EQ, general health, morale, quality of work life and performance, and significantly reduced stress as compared to those who did not join the programme.

It may be said that emotional intelligence could be a better predictor of performance than personality. Though controversial, there are many findings that show a small influence of IQ against a great impact of EQ on job performance.

Other studies have revealed that the most valued and productive employees are those who display high EI. The link between EI and work performance is more significant in 'people' jobs. Many of the tough challenges in any business involve people rather than technology. The ability to manage emotions and handle stress is a key aspect of emotional intelligence that is important for success.

XII. Emotional Intelligence and Stress Management

Darolia and Darolia (2005) studied the role of emotional intelligence in coping with stress and emotional control behaviour, and their findings are discussed in the following pages.

Sample

A sample of 400 adults (218 male and 182 female) in the age range of 25 to 40 years was drawn randomly from Kurukshetra City in Haryana, India, which covered people from all walks of life. The subjects were categorised into low and high emotional intelligence groups on the basis of lower and upper quartile of scores on Multidimensional Measure of Emotional Intelligence (MMEI). A total of 92 (50 male & 42 female) and 93 (52 male & 41 female) subjects were placed in low and high emotional intelligence groups. All the subjects were literate and covered a wide range of socio-economic status.

Measures

1. *Multidimensional Measure of Emotional Intelligence (MMEI):* The MMEI (Darolia, 2005) is comprised of 80 multiple-choice items distributed in five dimensions, each consisting 16 items. The five dimensions covered by MMEI, i.e., Self-awareness, Managing emotions, Motivating oneself, Empathy, and Handling relationships are thoroughly investigate.
2. *Coping Style Questionnaire (CSQ):* The CSQ (Roger et al., 1993) is a 41-item questionnaire, which taps four dimensions of coping style. There are nine items for rational coping, nine items for detached coping, 10 items for avoidance coping and 13 items for emotional coping.
3. *Emotional Control Questionnaire (ECQ):* The ECQ (Roger and Najarian, 1989) was designed to measure the tendency to inhibit the expression of emotional responses to stress and illness. Fifty-six items ECQ taps four dimensions of emotional control, i.e., Rehearsal, Emotional inhibition, Aggression control and Benign control.

Procedure

All the subjects were approached in residential localities and respective organisations to seek their consent for psychological testing. After seeking consent, they were contacted individually and all the three tests were administered in a single session with a rest of 5–10 minutes after each test. The testing was conducted in peaceful conditions with adequate sitting arrangement. The tests were administered in accordance with the procedure described by the respective test authors.

Results and Discussion

The means, standard deviations, and F-ratios for low and high emotional intelligence groups are shown in Table 5.11. It is clearly evident from the F-ratios that on 6 of the 8 measures of coping strategies low and high EI groups differ significantly. On both the measures of adaptive coping styles, i.e., rational coping and detached coping high EI subjects scored significantly higher than their low EI counterparts. Mean scores of high and low EI subjects on rational coping are 21.61 and 18.65 (F = 28.01, p < .0001) and on detached coping are 25.90 and 21.42 (F = 37.47, p < .0001), respectively. These results clearly suggest that high EI subjects predominantly use adaptive coping style on account of stressful life events. The findings reveal that emotionally intelligent people cope with stressful situation by realistically accepting it or sometimes successfully detaching themselves from stress generating events. The less involved they feel with the event more effectively they are able to cope. Interestingly, unlike low EI subjects high EI subjects don't feel helpless in coping with stressful events. High EI subjects scored low on avoidance coping (M = 11.77) as

TABLE 5.11: Means, SDs and F-ratios

Variable	Low EI Group Mean	SD	High EI Group Mean	SD	F	p
Rational Coping	18.65	4.30	21.61	3.24	28.01	<.0001
Detached Coping	21.42	5.73	25.90	4.10	37.47	<.0001
Avoidance Coping	17.17	4.22	11.77	3.11	98.26	<.00001
Emotional Coping	10.74	4.02	13.18	3.61	18.92	<.001
Rehearsal	6.64	2.81	6.28	2.76	.78	ns
Emotional Inhibition	6.47	1.97	6.39	2.16	.07	ns
Aggression Control	6.27	2.11	7.66	2.52	16.39	<.001
Benign Control	7.70	2.34	9.19	1.85	23.27	<.0001

compared to low EI subjects (M = 17.17) F = 98.26, p < .00001. It indicates that low EI subjects involve in maladaptive coping style by engaging in denial of stressful event or just giving up on account of stress. On the other hand, high EI subjects involve in expressing feelings and seeking emotional support from others. It is clearly reflected in higher mean score of high EI group on Emotional coping (M = 13.18) relative to those in low EI group (M = 10.74), F = 18.92, p < .001).

On two of the four measures of emotional control also low and high EI subjects differ significantly. Mean scores of low and high EI subjects on Aggression control are 6.27 and 7.66, respectively (F = 16.3, p < .001). It suggests that high emotionally intelligent people tend to inhibit the expression of their aggression and hostility successfully. Similarly, high EI subjects were found to be high in benign control, i.e., maintenance of patience on account of stress as compared to their low EI counterparts. Mean scores of low and high EI groups on benign control are 9.19 and 7.70, respectively (F = 23.27, p < .0001). These findings clearly establish that emotionally intelligent people, who are able to understand and recognise their emotions, manage themselves appropriately so that their impulsiveness and aggression is kept under control in stressful situations. However, on Rehearsal and Emotional inhibition components of emotional control strategy, low and high EI groups did not differ significantly. As indicated in the case of Emotional coping strategy, high EI people express their emotional feelings freely, therefore they don't tend to inhibit it.

It is assumed that if low and high emotional intelligence groups differ in coping strategies, linear combination of such coping strategies may predict EI group membership to a greater precision. With respect to this prediction, the obtained data were subjected to stepwise discriminator analysis. The results of discriminator analysis have been given in Table 5.12. A perusal of these results reveals that Avoidance coping, being the most potent predictor of group membership, entered the equation at step 1, F-to-enter equals to 98.26 (df = 1/183, p < .0001). At step 2 Rational coping entered the equation with F equal to 92.55 (df = 2/182, p < .0001). With the entry of two variables in the equation Wilk's Lambda reduced to 0.50. Lower Wilk's Lambda suggests more discrimination by the variables between the groups. Aggression control (F = 82.91, df = 3/181, p < .0001), Benign control (F = 67.79, df = 4/180, p < .0001), and Emotional coping (F = 57.65, df = 5/179, p < .0001) entered the equation at step 3, 4, and 5, respectively. Stepwise discriminator analysis identified these five coping strategies as most potent predictors of EI group membership. With the entry of these five variables Wilks' Lambda reduced to 0.38 indicating high degree of discrimination between the groups. The individual contribution of these coping strategies is indicated in terms of standardised canonical coefficient. Obviously, canonical coefficients of Avoidance coping is highest (.84) which took entry at step 1, and lowest for Emotional coping (.27) which was the last to enter the equation. The overall canonical correlation of these five variables with EI group membership equals to .785, which may be regarded as fairly high. These results clearly indicate high degree of classification accuracy based on identified set of discriminators.

TABLE 5.12: Summary of Stepwise Discriminator Analysis

Step No.	Variable Entered	Wilk's Lambda	F	Df	p	*Canonical Coefficient
1	Avoidance Coping	.65	98.26	1/183	<.0001	−.84
2	Rational Coping	.50	92.55	2/182	<.0001	.81
3	Aggression Control	.42	82.91	3/181	<.0001	.51
4	Benign Control	.40	67.79	4/180	<.0001	.27
5	Emotional Coping	.38	57.65	5/179	<.0001	.27

*Canonical correlation = .785.

The findings of comparisons of low and high emotional intelligence groups as well as multivariate discriminator functional analysis present an unequivocal evidence supporting the role of emotional intelligence in coping with stress. In the realm of stress and its coping, the range of variables that fall within the EI domain, its seems likely that at least some of them particularly managing emotions, empathy, and handling relationship are likely to boost effective coping. The results prove that EI helps in coping with stressful situations.

XIII. Managing Human Capital: An EQ Perspective

Shamira Malekar (2005) prepared a matrix of managing human capital from the perspective of emotional intelligence. She says that a superior's behaviour is acceptable to subordinates when viewed as a source of satisfaction and motivation. There is an expectation that the behaviour must be just and fair. The leader must facilitate, coach and reward effective performance. Management focuses on getting others to do what they would not do on their own. It involves thinking strategically, committing to self-improvement and lifelong learning, creating an innovative culture, helping others become leaders, developing a solution-focused workforce, disseminating information and instilling a mindset of continuous improvement. It focuses on building a solid, cohesive organisation that strives toward being an industry leader. This research focuses on three of the five parameters of Daniel Goleman's concept of emotional intelligence and directs its applicability to the workplace so that it becomes a more workable and enjoyable place.

Objectives

The objective of this study was to discuss the modalities of the three parameters of emotional intelligence under consideration and to provide a relationship between three of the five attributes of emotional intelligence and organisational effectiveness in managing employees.

The three parameters are *social relationships*, *empathy* and *motivation*. Social relationships are open systems that interact with their surroundings. Consequently, members in a social relationship should be aware of the nature of their environment, and their impact on other members both within and outside their own social environment. Empathy is the ability of organisations to realise that it is absolutely essential to understand and communicate with its employees in a way that makes them feel comfortable and share their grievances with experts in order to find solutions to their problems. This will help the employee to utilise his energy and competency in the most effective way that would be beneficial for both the employee and the organisation. The path to this begins with listening to the needs and requirements of employees, and their difficulties, all of which need to be addressed. Organisations realise that it is not sympathy, but empathy, that the employee expects. An empathetic individual listens carefully to what the other individual has to say and makes him feel comfortable. But nowhere in the conversation does he reveal to the troubled person that he is feeling sorry for the position he finds the individual in. He genuinely shows the troubled person his concern over the situation, but strongly restrains from showing himself as a person who pities the troubled individual. He only expresses his understanding of the problem and, at times, also offers probable solutions he finds best suitable at that time. Motivation means that the manager is to get people to contribute in activities that are considered to be of vital importance in accomplishment of the organisation's goals and objectives. Clearly, guiding people's activities in a desired manner requires knowing to the best of the manager's ability, what leads people to do things which motivate them. The corporate and its senior managers needs to motivate their employees and subordinates to do those things that they hope will satisfy the aforesaid drives of the employees and induce the subordinates to work in a desired manner. Thus, motivation is essentially the drive and effort to satisfy a particular want whereas satisfaction is the contentment after these wants and desires are satisfied.

Hence, emotional intelligence, or EI/EQ, has been one of the most underrated components of any organisation's HR plans. In most cases, HR departments speak of recruitment, training and even career planning, but very little revolves around the fitness or competencies of individuals to undertake the roles that are expected to deliver the best business results. Often training plans are made in a vacuum, considering only the desirable aspect of the business without mapping the competencies of individuals and, in some cases, it may be the reverse, which is in fact a far worse situation.

It is important that the various roles in an organisation be mapped vis-à-vis their competency requirements on to the EI grid of Social Interaction, Empathy and Motivation. Roles defined at lower levels in organisations are typically task oriented and the component of the generic competencies tends to be low. But as we go up the hierarchical ladder, the relevance of the EI parameters starts to have increasing importance. Job design typically is the combination of a role, its context and the expectations of that role, its business outcome and the competencies that are required of the person to make this role a success. These competencies can be generic or functional. The latter has more to do with knowledge and its application. The former is linked to the EI parameters that define effectiveness of the holder of these generic competencies.

Individuals who occupy job positions are a bundle of behaviour, attitude and skills. They are not at the most supreme position in each parameter that we choose to define but in most cases the sum may be greater than the individual parts. Organisations define generic competencies as achievement orientation, planning and analysis, business orientation, communicating and influencing, teamwork, leadership and interpersonal effectiveness. The competency scores under these broad heads need not be at the best of each individual competency. The key is in the permutation and combination of these competencies that makes for the best fit for organisational positions. That best fit is best captured by mapping these competencies on to the EI parameters of social behaviour, empathy and motivation.

It is thus possible to draw up a framework for each competency versus the three EI parameters as follows:

Competency	Impacting EQ Parameter		
	Social Interaction	Empathy	Motivation
Achievement Orientation	High	Low	High
Planning and Analysis	Low	Low	High
Business Perspective	High	Low	Low
Communicating and Influencing	High	High	High
Teamwork	High	High	High
Leadership	High	High	High
Interpersonal Effectiveness	High	High	Low

This matrix can be used at the time of evaluation of a candidate for a higher position as well as in a performance appraisal situation. The disadvantage of the approach is in the amount of measurement involved and the plethora of tools that may need to be deployed to get the most effective results. This model is not the simplest of ones to be put into practice, but once individuals in organisations have been mapped on this matrix it is also possible to work on the combinations of people that are likely to work most effectively in teams and in pairs as the superior and the subordinate. The results of such an application are also likely to hold for a good period of time and the need for very frequent recalibration may not arise at all.

Conclusion

There is rich potential in the application of EI to the management of human capital. Very often, organisational systems fail to recognise the softer facets of people and slot people into assignments for which they are inherently incapable. Such situations result in conflict and behaviour that is at times uncondonable and bitter. Job design with an eye on the emotional intelligence content of a role is as important as the definition of role, the competencies it requires and the clean execution of tasks. A successful integration of these elements can lead to far greater organisational success stories than those on board today and probably far healthier work environments in these organisations as well.

XIV. The Making of an EQ Test

The EQ test provided in this book has been developed by Dr Dalip Singh and Professor N.K. Chadha. Some of the readers may be interested in knowing how this test was developed. We are providing details of the procedure that was adopted to finalise the test. This exercise usually is a cumbersome process involving collecting a plethora of data from targeted subjects and making a detailed statistical analysis. The most important step in making a psychological test is its standardisation. This involves situation selection, situation analysis and critically evaluating the reliability and validity of a test on given parameters. Accordingly, the following steps were initiated to finalise the present EQ test.

Situation Selection

The subject EQ test was drawn up by compiling real-life situations experienced by individuals in their day-to-day life. The situations were selected to avoid response bias such as 'faking-good' or 'social desirability tendency' by the respondents. This tendency refers to the inherent tendency of an individual to conform to social norms. Psychologists today unanimously hold that the tendency of the individual to give socially desirable rather than true answers to emotional inventories lessens their usefulness. There are ordinarily three approaches to control the social desirability of an emotional inventory. One way is to arrange the situations in an inventory in such a way that the subject is forced to choose between two equally desirable options. But the forced choice technique has its disadvantage because it seems to create more problems than it solves. The second way is to use an independent social desirability scale and the score on this scale may be correlated with scores on other inventories to give an index for this tendency. The third way is to have such situations in the inventory that are relatively neutral with respect to such desirability and thereby avoid a response bias. In the present context, only such situations that have been deemed relatively neutral with regard to social desirability tendency were introduced. In order to achieve this, the situations were passed on to five judges/experts on psychological, behavioural and emotional aspects, with a request to rate each situation on a nine-point rating scale ranging from 'extremely desirable' through 'neutral' to 'extremely undesirable'. A modified version of Edward's instructions given to judges/experts is given below.

> In this test booklet, you will find 45 real-life situations from the immediate environment regarding people's liking, disliking, character, way of thinking and doing tasks. These situations reflect some areas of emotional intelligence

such as self-awareness, self-regulation, handling relationships, motivation, conflict resolution and stress management. We are not interested in knowing whether the situation applies or does not apply to you personally. You are to rate the situations in terms of whether you consider them desirable or undesirable in others. Kindly make sure that you have rated each situation. Please read each situation carefully and rate them on the scale given below as to how socially desirable or undesirable they are if applied to other people.

Rating	Meaning of rating
1	Extremely undesirable
2	Strongly undesirable
3	Moderately undesirable
4	Mildly undesirable
5	Neutral
6	Mildly desirable
7	Moderately desirable
8	Strongly desirable
9	Extremely desirable

After the experts had rated the situations, the ratings were converted into scores. The mean value of each situation computed on the basis of the experts' 'ratings' on a 9-point scale constituted the social desirability scale values for each situation. The mean of the scale was, theoretically, 5. The items that had ratings of 1–3 and 7–9 were rejected as they were higher on socially undesirable as well as socially desirable dimensions; hence ratings of 4–6 were retained. According to Edward, the situations having social desirability scale values around the mean of the social desirability continuum are less prone to social desirability tendencies than those that fall outside this range. As such, it was decided to retain only those situations whose average experts' ratings was more than 5. Two situations were consequently dropped. The remaining 43 situations were retained after rejection on the basis of social desirability components.

Item Analysis

While analysing items of any psychometric tests, two types of information are usually needed: index of situation difficulty and index of situation validity. The question of *situation difficulty* does not arise in emotional inventories, as there is no 'pass' or 'fail' in response. To determine the index of *situation validity*, before administering the scale to subjects for situation analysis, a clear instruction in very simple language was also prepared and printed on the first page of the scale so that each subject was able to follow them before responding to situations. Subjects were asked to respond to the situations by putting a tick mark under 'yes' if they agreed and under 'no' if they disagreed. Two techniques were used for the purpose of item analysis: (*a*) skewness (percentage of responses) and (*b*) Chi-square (discrimination indices).

(A) SKEWNESS

For the purpose of skewness, 43 situations were applied to a sample of 900 respondents from different walks of life. Based on the reponses given in the four categories, percentages of responses were calculated, and the results are presented below:

Frequency of Response (Skewness) N = 900
Response (percentage)

Item No.	a	b	c	d	Decision
1	27	24	29	21	Retained
2	28	25	23	24	Retained
3	36	17	11	36	**Rejected**
4	26	25	27	22	Retained
5	25	25	30	20	Retained
6	9	31	10	50	**Rejected**
7	27	22	22	29	Retained
8	28	21	24	27	Retained
9	25	26	24	25	Retained
10	23	27	25	25	Retained
11	7	13	35	45	**Rejected**
12	26	26	24	24	Retained
13	20	25	25	30	Retained
14	24	26	27	23	Retained
15	26	30	24	20	Retained
16	23	27	26	22	Retained
17	11	9	12	68	**Rejected**

Contd.

Contd.

18	13	12	61	14	**Rejected**
19	27	27	26	20	Retained
20	31	23	24	22	Retained
21	29	25	23	23	Retained
22	26	28	21	25	Retained
23	11	59	18	12	**Rejected**
24	24	27	23	26	Retained
25	25	26	24	25	Retained
26	11	9	8	7	**Rejected**
27	25	26	24	25	Retained
28	63	11	12	14	**Rejected**
29	30	20	25	25	Retained
30	63	7	10	20	**Rejected**
31	20	50	25	5	**Rejected**
32	30	20	30	20	Retained
33	9	9	12	70	**Rejected**
34	25	30	20	25	Retained
35	12	13	60	68	**Rejected**
36	27	24	26	23	Retained
37	64	11	11	14	**Rejected**
38	15	55	15	15	**Rejected**
39	25	29	21	25	Retained
40	8	12	10	70	**Rejected**
41	23	27	24	26	Retained
42	15	10	15	60	**Rejected**
43	23	29	27	21	Retained

On the basis of the normality of the responses, the situations that did not fit into the normality were rejected and those that fit in were retained. Hence, 27 situations were retained and 16 were rejected.

(B) CHI-SQUARE

Following Kelley's instructions, the scale was administered on an unselected sample from different professions of 300 (males and females) for the purpose of situation analysis. The samples were drawn from different sections of the society. The age range of the subjects was 18 years to 50 years. They were managers, executives from public/private sector undertakings, doctors, senior government officers, entrepreneurs and industrialists from private sector, teachers from colleges and universities, and from other professions such as nursing, accountancy, engineering, banking, medicine, information technology, judiciary, police, business, politics and insurance. On the basis of the total scores of each dimension, the 27th percentile and 73rd percentile were computed which constituted the lower and the upper groups comprising 81 subjects each. Chi-square for each item was computed from the phi-coefficient. The phi-correlation and chi-square values with significant levels for each item are presented below:

Situation Number	Phi-correlation	Chi-square	Level of Significance	Remarks
1	0.33	17.64	0.01	Accepted
2	0.10	1.62	NS*	**Rejected**
3	0.11	01.96	NS*	**Rejected**
4	0.22	11.81	0.01	Accepted
5	0.14	03.18	NS*	**Rejected**
6	0.24	09.33	0.01	Accepted
7	0.25	10.13	0.01	Accepted
8	0.18	05.24	NS*	**Rejected**
9	0.39	24.64	0.01	Accepted
10	0.29	13.62	0.01	Accepted
11	0.20	06.48	0.05	Accepted
12	0.19	05.84	NS*	**Rejected**
13	0.29	13.62	0.01	Accepted
14	0.11	01.96	NS*	**Rejected**
15	0.34	18.73	0.01	Accepted
16	0.26	10.95	0.01	Accepted
17	0.09	01.31	NS*	**Rejected**
18	0.30	14.58	0.01	Accepted
19	0.25	10.13	0.01	Accepted
20	0.10	01.62	NS*	**Rejected**
21	0.22	07.84	0.01	Accepted
22	0.31	15.57	0.01	Accepted
23	0.29	13.62	0.01	Accepted

*Not significant.

The situations having non-significant chi-square values were dropped from the scale at this stage. Two levels of significant that are 5 per cent and 1 per cent were taken as the criterion for dropping the situations. With this, eight situations were dropped and, in the final EQ scale, 15 situations were retained.

RELIABILITY OF THE TEST

The concept of reliability occupies a central place in psychological testing. According to Stanley, reliability is the first and primary requisite of any measuring instrument. Reliability refers to internal consistency and temporal stability of the measurement. Both consistency and stability are intimately related, but are used in different contexts. When the test yields consistent results upon testing and retesting, it is said to have temporal stability. More approximately, consistency means to what extent the test is internally consistent when administered once. Both stability and consistency are incorporated under the single term, reliability.

For the present scale, test-retest and split-half reliabilities were computed. To find the 'retest reliability', a sample of 150 (males and females) was taken. A sample was drawn from different streams of the population, as mentioned earlier. The present scale was administered twice with a time interval of 15 days to the same sample. Pearsonian 'r' was computed between the two sets of measures to indicate the stability coefficient of the scale. The retest reliability for the test was found to be 0.94. The 'split-half' is another method of estimating reliability coefficient. It measures internal consistency of test scores. The data collected in the case of retest on 150 subjects was taken for split-half reliability. The whole data was divided into two halves, namely, 'even' and 'odd' as well as 'first half and second half' for the total scale. The split-half reliability in the case of odd-even items was 0.89 and for the first half and second half was 0.91. Both reliability coefficients are significantly higher, which indicate that the present EQ scale enjoys high reliability.

VALIDITY OF THE TEST

In psychological measurement, the problem of validity arises because the measurement instruments are indirect. As these instruments are indirect measures, it is very essential to gather sufficient evidence to support that the test measures the traits of characteristics for which it was designed. Validity means truthfulness or usefulness of the test. Thus, validity of a test is concerned with *what* it measures and *how* well it measures. A test stands valid against some independent criteria. Validity is not governed by an 'all-or-none' law; it is a relative term. The test is valid for a particular purpose and in a particular situation only. Moreover, validity is not fixed on unitary characteristics of the test; new validity indices must be sought. In the present case, validity was determined with the help of two techniques (*a*) face validity, and (*b*) empirical validity. Face validity is confirmed for the test as seen by the agreement of the five experts who found the test valid. The empirical validity of the scale was assessed by correlating the scale with 'external criteria'. The external criteria taken in the present study was a sample of 60 subjects. The test, designed by Daniel Goleman, and the present scale was administered to these 60 subjects. The scores obtained from both tests were correlated to determine the validity index. The validity was found to be 0.92, which indicates that the present EQ scale is valid. Further, the present scale was co-related with the emotional intelligence test developed by Chadha (2005) on 60 subjects to determine the validity index. The validity was found to be 0.78, which indicates that the present test is valid.

Readers may note that like any other psychological concept, the EQ test also has its share of criticism. Some psychologists have doubts about the authenticity of EQ measurement. They say that the idea that you can measure emotional intelligence as you can IQ, is very misleading. Emotional skills are slippery and relative in a way that IQ is not. They believe that it may not be entirely possible to measure EQ characteristics such as anger, frustration, love and empathy. For example, your communication ability with someone you know is different from your communication ability with a stranger, and each relationship will have its own characteristic emotional communication. If you try to measure empathy, your measurement will depend on whom you are empathetic towards. However, psychologists have established that it is possible to measure emotional characteristics of an individual by using scientific tools.

XV. Other Research Studies

Benefits in Life

- There is convincing evidence that psychological states do affect health. Depression, grieving, pessimism all seem to worsen health in both the short run and long term (Martin Seligman, *Learned Optimism*, 1998).
- Success depends on 'mature adaptations' including altruism, humor, self-management, and optimism/anticipation. People do change over time (George Vaillant, *Adaptation to Life*, 1995).
- As much as 80 per cent of adult 'success' comes from EQ (Daniel Goleman 1996).
- 75 per cent of careers are derailed for reasons related to emotional incompetencies, including inability to handle interpersonal problems; unsatisfactory team leadership during times of difficulty or conflict; or inability to adapt to change or elicit trust (The Centre for Creative Leadership 1994).
- 85-95 per cent of the difference between a 'good leader' and an 'excellent leader' is due to emotional intelligence (Goleman 1998).
- Impulsive boys are 3-6 times as likely to be violent as adolescents, and impulsive girls are 3 times more likely to get pregnant in adolescence (Block 1995).
- Optimism is a skill that can be taught. Optimists are more motivated, more successful, have higher levels of achievement, plus significantly better physical and mental health (Seligman 1995).
- The chronically sad/depressed are 2 times as likely to contract a major debilitating disease (McEwen, Stillar 1993; Robertson & Ritz 1990).

- People who accurately perceive others' emotions are better able to handle changes and build stronger social networks.
- Children's abilities to handle frustration, control emotions, and get along with other people is a better predictor of success than IQ.
- Emotions and reason are intertwined, and both are critical to problem solving (Damasio 1997).
- Social and emotional abilities were four times more important than IQ in determining professional success and prestige.

Benefits in School

- After EQ training, discipline referrals to the principals dropped by 95 per cent (Johnson & Johnson 1994).
- Social and emotional skills create higher achievement (Ornstein 1986; Lakoff 1980).
- Improved emotional skills increase 'on task' behaviours (Rosenfield 1991).
- Increased social and emotional skills reduce discipline problems (Doyle 1986).
- The basic unit of human memory is information in context connected to feelings. This means that how someone learns is as important as what someone learns (Maurice Elias 1999).
- Emotions give a more activated and chemically stimulated brain, which helps us recall things better (Cahill et al. 1994).
- After 30 social-emotional lessons, hostility decreased and pro-social behaviour increased (Grossman, *Second Step*).
- EQ training increases focus, learning, collaboration, improves classroom relationships, and decreases both negative 'put downs' and violence (Anabel Jensen, *Self-Science Pilot Study*, 2001).
- Emotions are more important and powerful to the brain than higher-order thinking skills (Eric Jensen, *Brain Based Learning*).

- People who have poor abilities at reading body language are less academically successful (Katz and Hoover 1997).
- Children with highly developed social skills perform better academically than peers who lack these skills (Grossman et al. 1997).
- Students who are anxious or depressed earn lower grades/lower achievement scores, and are more likely to repeat a grade (Kovics and Baatraens 1994).
- Children's written/spoken narratives are more accurate, detailed, and coherent when preceded by emotional content (Liwag and Stein 1995, cited in Frey 1999).
- Emotions are crucial to sensory development because they facilitate the storage and recall of information (Rosenfield 1988).
- Stress and threat cause the brain to downshift; this reduces the opportunity for neuron growth and causes learning to be inhibited (Ornstein and Sobel 1987).
- Low levels of empathy are associated with poor school achievement (Nowicki and Duke 1992, cited in Frey 1999).
- Children who respond to setbacks with hope and resiliency vs. anger and hopelessness achieve higher academic and social success (Dweck 1996).
- Students who believe their teachers support and care about them are more engaged with their work (Skinner and Belmont 1993); they value their work more, and have higher academic goals (Goodnow 1993, cited in Frey 1999).
- Children who are able to delay gratification are more popular, earn better grades, and had an average of 210 more points on their SAT tests (Shoda, Mischel and Peake 1990).
- Scores on a test of hope are more accurate than the SAT at predicting college grades (Snyder, 1991); the same is true of a test on optimism.
- Teachers can help students lessen their frustrations, prevent behavioural problems, and accelerate learning by providing students with information and skills to make appropriate choices (Dewhurst, 1991; Meyer, 1990).

Benefits in Business

- The reasons for losing customers and clients are 70 per cent EQ-related (e.g., didn't like that company's customer service) (Forum Corporation on Manufacturing and Service Companies 1989–95).
- 50 per cent of time wasted in business is due to lack of trust (John O. Whitney, Director, Deming Centre for Quality Management).
- In one year, the US Air Force invested less than $10,000 for emotional competence testing and saved $2,760,000 in recruitment ('How Do You Feel', *Fastcompany*, June 2000).
- In a multinational consulting firm, partners who showed high emotional intelligence (EQ) competencies earned 139 per cent more than the lower EQ partners (Boyatzis 1999).
- American Express tested emotional competence training on Financial Advisors; trained advisors increased business 18.1 per cent compared to 16.2 per cent, and nearly 90 per cent of those who took the training reported significant improvements in their sales performance. Now all incoming advisors receive four days of emotional competence training ('How Do You Feel', *Fastcompany* June 2000).
- After supervisors in a manufacturing plant received training in emotional competencies, lost-time accidents were reduced by 50 per cent, formal grievances were reduced from an average of 15 per year to 3 per year, and the plant exceeded productivity goals by $250,000 (Pesuric & Byham 1996).
- Top performing sales clerks are 12 times more productive than those at the bottom and 85 per cent more productive than an average performer. About one-third of this difference is due to technical skill and cognitive ability while two-thirds is due to emotional competence (Goleman 1998).
- UCLA research indicates that only 7 per cent of leadership success is attributable to intellect; 93 per cent of success comes from trust, integrity, authenticity, honesty, creativity, presence, and resilience (cited in Cooper and Sawaf 1996).

- At L'Oreal, sales agents selected on the basis of certain emotional competencies significantly outsold salespeople selected using the company's old selection procedure by $91,370, for a net revenue increase of $2,558,360. Salespeople selected on the basis of emotional competence also had 63 per cent less turnover during the first year (Spencer & Spencer 1993; Spencer, McClelland & Kelner 1997, cited in Cherniss 2000).
- The most effective leaders in the US Navy were warmer, more outgoing, emotionally expressive, dramatic, and sociable (Bachman 1988, cited in Cherniss 2000).

Workers with high work pressures and poor time management skills are twice as likely to miss work; employees who have strong self-management skills cope better with work pressures (Essi Systems 1997).

# Guidelines for Training and Development

> Everyone prefers to feel important, needed, useful, successful, proud, respected, rather than unimportant, interchangeable, anonymous, wasted, unused, expendable, disrespected.
>
> —N.K. Chadha

The Work Psychology and Human Resources Forum (WPHRF) (2006) has prepared guidelines for developing EQ in organisations, based on the best available knowledge on how to promote emotional learning. This includes defining and simplifying training procedures and processes. Many business leaders agree with the basic message that success is strongly influenced by personal qualities such as perseverance, self-control and skill in getting along with others. These leaders cite the example of 'super salespersons' who have an uncanny ability to sense what is most important to customers and develop a trusting relationship with them. They also quote the example of customer service employees who excel at helping angry customers calm down and be more reasonable regarding their problems with the product or service. They also point to brilliant executives who do everything well except get along with people, or to managers who are technically brilliant but cannot handle stress, and who stall because of such deficiencies.

> 'EQ consultants can raise the emotional intelligence of employers/employees by giving them effective EQ training.'

But what of the many employees who lack these important emotional competencies? Is it possible for them to become more emotionally competent? Many business leaders are less certain about this question. For instance, when questioned about the importance of emotional intelligence at work, the dean of a major business school in Delhi enthusiastically agreed that it was crucial. But when he was asked to describe how his school improved the emotional intelligence of MBA students, he said, 'we don't do anything. I don't think that our students' emotional intelligence can be improved by the time they come here. They're already adults, and these qualities are developed early in life.'

On the other hand, there are those who claim that they can raise the emotional intelligence of employees by giving them effective EQ training. Scores of EQ consultants are organising workshops and seminars designed to help employees become more emotionally competent and socially skilled. A growing body of research on emotional learning and behaviour modification indicates that it is possible to help employers and employees of any age to become more emotionally intelligent at work. This is substantiated by research on training and development, organisational behaviour, personnel management, human resources management, etc. For instance, take the case of the engineer whose career stagnated because he was shy, introverted and totally absorbed in the technical aspects of his job. Through emotional learning, it would have been possible for him to understand that it would be beneficial for him to frequently consult other people, make connections and forge relationships. But merely knowing that he should do these things may not have enabled him to do them. The ability to do these things calls for emotional competence.

Emotional incompetence is often due to deeply ingrained habits learned early on in life. These automatic habits are set in place as a normal part of living, as experience shapes the brain. As people acquire their habitual repertoire of thought, feeling and action, the neural connections that support these are strengthened, becoming the dominant pathways for nerve impulses. Connections that are unused become weak, while those that are used repeatedly become increasingly stronger. When these habits have been overly heavily learned, the underlying neural circuitry becomes the brain's default option at any given moment, and makes people do things automatically and spontaneously, often without being aware why they choose to do so. Thus, for the shy engineer, lack of confidence is a habit that must be overcome and replaced with a new habit—self-confidence.

The WPHRF says that with effective training, emotional learning can be mastered. The training process includes four basic phases. The first phase occurs even before the individual begins formal training. This initial phase, which is crucial for effective social and emotional learning, involves preparation for change, and it occurs at both the organisational and individual levels. In the second phase, the training focuses on the change process itself. This includes the processes that help people change the way in which they view the world and deal with its social and emotional demands. The third phase, transfer and maintenance, focuses on what happens after formal training experience has been gained. The final phase involves evaluation. Given the current state of knowledge about emotional learning, the complexity of programmes designed to promote such learning and the unevenness in the effectiveness of existing ones, evaluation should always be part of the process. Each phase will be examined in depth to obtain greater insight into the processes involved.

PHASE ONE: PREPARATION FOR CHANGE

Motivation is especially important in social and emotional learning. Such learning can be challenging for employees who have already established a way of relating to others and to themselves. It is important to be strongly committed to the change process for an extended period of time. So, what can managers and trainers do to increase learners' motivation prior to the onset of the change process? Several guidelines are available to address this question.

- **Assessing the organisation's needs** Good training begins with a proper needs assessment. For emotional training, there are two particular challenges that must be addressed at this point in the process. First, many employees in an organisation may be sceptical about the link between emotional intelligence and work performance. In a large financial services company, for instance, there was considerable scepticism regarding the value of training in 'emotional competence'. Top executives were shown the results of a study which revealed that financial advisors who were able to cope better with the emotional aspects of work involving clients sold more life insurance policies. Once they saw the connection between this particular type of emotional competence and the bottom line, they encouraged advisors to participate in emotional competency training programmes.

The second challenge is to identify the emotional competencies that are important for being successful. Sometimes, crucial ones are easily overlooked. For instance, in a particular airline, an initial needs assessment began with a consideration of the airline's business strategy. Since all airlines are similar in price structure, any competitive advantage will depend, in particular, on how well passengers are treated by the airline personnel. As a result, the way in which the airline's flight attendants/airhostesses handled passengers became the focus of its training efforts. The results revealed that top performers exhibited two types of competencies: self-management skills (resilience, efficiency and adaptability) and interpersonal skills (caring for and managing customers well and teamwork). However, two other competencies—self-awareness and empathy—support self-management and interpersonal competencies, hence the need to include these also in the training programmes. A careful assessment of the work situation, informed by an understanding of the nature of emotional competence, enabled the consultant to identify both the surface level and deeper competencies that affected performance.

- **Assessing personal strengths and limitations** There are two challenges in the assessment of the emotional competence of employees. First, people are usually less aware of skill weaknesses in the social and emotional domains. They may realise, for example, the difficult and frustrating interpersonal aspects of leading a work group. But they may not be able to pinpoint the emotional skills that are needed to improve their functioning in this area. They are probably even less aware of the underlying attitudes and ways of thinking which lead them into trouble, or how such ways of thinking trigger complex emotional response patterns that impede their effectiveness in dealing with difficult employees, customers or co-workers.

Second, these competencies are primarily manifested in social interactions. Therefore, the best approach is usually one that involves ratings by experts who interact with them. However, personal beliefs, motives and feelings of experts may influence their ratings of emotional competence. The boss's view of a manager's self-awareness or ability to empathise may vary widely from the perspective of the manager's peers and subordinates. The best assessment approach to emotional learning is thus usually based on multiple ratings done from multiple perspectives, such as boss, peer and subordinate ratings.

- **Providing feedback with care** Motivation for change can be enhanced when employees are given feedback on assessment results. There are, however, many pitfalls in providing feedback on emotional competence as these competencies are closely linked to employees' identity and self-esteem. It is one thing, for example, to be told that you need to improve your driving, but it is quite another to be told that you need to improve your self-confidence. If the feedback is not provided with sensitivity and skill, employees often become defensive.

  Employees are more likely to respond positively to feedback when they trust and respect the person who gives it. They are also more likely to be motivated to change when they believe that the feedback is constructive and accurate, and when they are supported in their efforts to identify the specific steps that they can take to improve themselves.

Employees need sufficient time to think about the feedback and its implications. In emotional development efforts, it is especially important that the feedback is given in an atmosphere of confidence and trust.
- **Maximising learner choice** Employees are more motivated to change if they can freely choose to do so. In emotional training, in particular, choice is very important.

  As these competencies are closely linked to the essence of what makes employees the people they are, it makes sense if they are free to choose whether or not to participate in such training. What is more important is that the choice is real. If they are given a choice but not assigned to the training they initially chose, they will be less motivated to learn than those who are given no choice.
- **Encouraging participation** Emotional learning is perceived as a 'soft skill'. Employees may decide not to participate in it unless they are convinced that the organisation's management is strongly endorsing it. The words and actions of supervisors are especially important. Employees are more likely to participate in development activity if their supervisors support it. For instance, in a large financial services company, a training programme on emotional competence was popular because several regional vice presidents encouraged management groups to participate and also attended the programme along with them.

  The same was true of a programme designed to teach airline crew the emotional skills that would enable them to work better as a team. When senior management demonstrated true commitment to the programme by providing intensive and recurrent training, there was greater acceptance of it among the airline crew.
- **Linking learning goals to personal values** Supervisors will be more motivated to learn and change if they believe that by doing so they will achieve the goals they value. For instance, while instructing airline crew on how to work better as a team in the cockpit, it was observed that it was more effective to teach them 'how to get a team off to a good

start' and 'how to address conflicts among members constructively', rather than to instruct them about 'behavioural styles'.

While most salient personal values are often work related, this need not be necessarily true. For example, attempts to motivate learners by demonstrating that the training will contribute to career success may be futile if success has no meaning for them. Fortunately, there are numerous other incentives for emotional learning. In a popular emotional competence programme, for example, many participants reported that the skills they learned were as valuable in managing relationships at home as they were at work.

- **Adjusting expectations** Expectations about performance can become self-fulfilling prophecies. Employees who are confident that they will succeed in a training programme will not only be more motivated, but also more successful. Unfortunately, as far as emotional learning is concerned, many employees are sceptical about the prospects of improving emotional intelligence. Those who find emotional problems challenging are particularly dubious about their ability to improve. To maximise motivation, learners need to believe that not only does emotional competence lead to valued outcomes, but that it can also be improved. Furthermore, they need to have a realistic expectation of what the training process involves.
- **Recognising readiness to change** Research on a wide variety of behaviour change programmes reveals that employees pass through several stages of readiness for change before they are actually ready to make a true commitment. In the first stage, they deny that they have any need for change. In the next stage, they begin to realise that they need to improve, but they are not sure that anything can be done about their problems and they put off making a decision. In the third stage, they recognise that there is a problem and that there are ways of dealing with it, but they have not formulated a concrete plan of action. It is not until the fourth stage that they are ready to act. It is at this stage that they have a concrete plan and

they put it into action. Before the training begins (or towards the beginning of the training), trainers should, ideally, assess the level of readiness of each potential participant. On the basis of such an assessment they should design appropriate intervention, which will vary for people at different levels of readiness.

Phase Two: Training

Motivation in emotional learning continues to be an important issue during the training phase. The amount of time, effort and potential threats to self-esteem during emotional learning indicate that trainers should monitor every employee's motivation and intervene continually to bolster it. One of the most important factors influencing motivation during the training phase is the relationship between the trainer and the learner.

- **Fostering a positive relationship between the trainer and the learner** The relationship between the trainer and the learner is critically important. For instance, in an emotional learning programme designed to teach assertiveness, participants are less likely to drop out and will show more positive change at the end of the programme if they enjoy a positive relationship with the trainer. Trainers who are empathic, warm and genuine (all attributes of emotional intelligence) develop more positive relationships with participants in behaviour change programmes, and are more likely to be successful. Trainers who use a confrontational style only succeed in making participants more resistant.
- **Maximising self-directed change** Employees are more likely to develop emotional competence when they decide which competencies to work on and set their own goals. Training programmes on emotional competence also benefit when the trainer adapts the training to match employees' needs, goals and learning style preferences. For instance, in a stress management programme, participants were taught a variety of

approaches to relaxation. They were then encouraged to try all options and then select the best one for themselves. If none of them worked well, they were encouraged to try other approaches to manage stress, such as improving their time management skills. The basic message of the programme was that since people differ, there is no single approach to managing stress that works well for everyone.

- **Setting clear goals** Social and emotional learning can be enhanced by setting specific and clear goals. A goal such as 'learn how to listen better to subordinates' is likely to be less effective than one which advocates 'using active listening at least three times each day for three weeks'. Specific and challenging goals support social and emotional learning because they maximise self-efficacy, mastery and motivation. The most effective trainers are able to help learners set clear and challenging goals without infringing on their sense of ownership of the goals.

- **Breaking goals into manageable steps** For many employees, trying to bring about even modest improvements in emotional competence can be frustrating. Although challenging goals are more motivating than simple ones, it also helps if goals are attainable. When employees attain goals, their self-efficacy increases, leading to the setting of new and more challenging goals. For instance, an MBA student lacked the self-confidence necessary to approach people for a part-time job. The larger goal of developing self-confidence was overwhelming (as also vague), and he was helped to break it into smaller, more realistic action steps. The first step was to update his resume, which was easy and could be done without seeking any external assistance. The subsequent steps, which were increasingly more difficult, included contacting the chairman of the finance department by the following month to request a meeting, discussing various opportunities with the chairman, and also with his mentor, a local executive. As a final step, the student was to scan the local job advertisements and call to apply for promising jobs. In this way, the goal of increasing self-confidence became

attainable, and steady progress was made and success, rather than frustration and failure, characterised the process.
- **Maximising opportunities to practice** The relationship between practice and learning is one of the oldest and most well established principles in psychology and management. Emotional learning calls for more frequent practice than any other type of learning because old, ineffective neural connections need to be weakened and new, more effective ones established. Such a process requires repetition over a prolonged period of time. Learners need to practice on the job for such a transfer to occur.
- **Providing frequent feedback on practice** Feedback is important during the change process as an indicator of whether the employee is on track. It also helps to sustain motivation, as feedback can be highly reinforcing. Feedback is especially useful in emotional learning because learners often have trouble recognising how their emotional behaviour manifests itself. In fact, because self-awareness is a core competence, those who need the most help in emotional competence programmes may be particularly weak in this area. Thus, they should be given even more focused and sustained feedback as they practise new behaviours.
- **Relying on experiential methods** More active, concrete, experiential methods in emotional learning such as role play, group discussions and simulations, usually work better than the lecture method or assigned reading.

In order to re-programme neural circuits, it is important to actually engage in the desired pattern of thought, feeling and action. The lecture method is effective to increase employees' understanding of emotional intelligence, but experiential methods are essential to effect real behaviour change. A study of managerial and sales training programmes launched in a large corporation demonstrated the superiority of experiential methods in social and emotional learning. Programmes that used experiential methods led to twice as much improvement in performance (as rated by supervisors and peers) as did others.

- **Building in support** Change is enhanced through ongoing support from individuals and small groups. Such support is especially valuable for those who are trying to enhance their emotional competence. Coaches, mentors as well as individuals who are going through the same change process, can help sustain a person's hopes and motivation. Emotional training programmes are usually more effective when they encourage the formation of groups where people give each other support throughout the change effort.

  In a stress management programme designed for a group of middle-level managers in a high profile firm, trainers assigned participants to a 'support group' early in the first session. All small group work during the course of the programme took place in these support groups, and facilitators included activities that helped group members get to know one another better.

  Participants were also encouraged to interact with others in their support groups in between sessions and after the programme had formally ended. Participants reported that the discussions they had in their support groups about work style and priorities were the most important factors that helped them to make positive changes in their work.

- **Using models** Modelling of the desired behaviour is particularly valuable in emotional learning. It is not possible to learn to solve quadratic equations by watching someone else do so, but a great deal can be learnt about how to discuss a conflict with a co-worker by observing a model. Learning is further enhanced when trainers encourage and help learners to study, analyse and emulate the models.

- **Enhancing insight** Even though experiential interventions seem to be especially productive in emotional learning, insight can also play a useful role. Insight serves as a natural link between situations, thoughts and feelings. It enhances self-awareness, the cornerstone of emotional intelligence, and often paves the way for meaningful behaviour change.

  The most effective training combines experiential methods with insight development. For instance, in one programme managers were taught to be more aware of how their employees irritated them and become more effective in setting limits with employees. The trainer began the session by showing an excerpt from a popular comedy film in which one character continually annoyed another by infringing on his personal space in numerous ways. After screening the film, the trainer helped the participants to shift the focus from the film to themselves, and they began to see how they had often allowed some of their employees to bother them in similar annoying ways. After gaining greater insight into their own emotional reactions, the participants were ready to learn the skills that could help them to deal with such annoying behaviours.

- **Preventing relapse** The essence of preventing relapse is to prepare employees mentally to face slips, to recognise at the outset that setbacks are a normal part of the change process. Relapse prevention is especially important in emotional learning because participants attempting to develop such competencies are likely to encounter many setbacks as they strive to apply new behaviours on the job. Without adequate preparation for such setbacks, they can easily become discouraged and give up before the task of neural relearning has reached the point where the new, learned response becomes an automatic one.

    For example, in one programme, a trainer led participants through a discussion about a hypothetical situation in which a participant who had followed all the rules for effective, supportive feedback received an angry response from a staff member. The trainer then asked the group to describe how they would feel in such a situation and to examine what they could do to overcome this particular obstacle. The trainer commended the participants for their ideas on how to bounce back from such a setback. Later, the trainer asked the participants to write down on one side of a sheet of paper, descriptions of setbacks they might have encountered when they tried to apply a skill they had learned, and to generate possible solutions for overcoming such setbacks on the other side of the paper. The participants then shared these strategies with the rest of the group.

Emotional competence training further involves step-by-step learning of the following aspects.

Training should focus on the competencies needed most for excellence in a given job or role. Experience shows that training in irrelevant competencies is pointless. Training should be designed on the basis of a systematic needs assessment. Further, employees' profiles of strengths and weaknesses should be prepared to identify the areas in which they need to improve. It is futile to send employees for training in competencies they already have or do not need. As mentioned earlier, people have varying levels of readiness, hence it is important to assess their readiness; if someone lacks readiness, cultivating it should be the initial focus.

If employees are unmotivated, training will lack effectiveness. It should therefore be made clear to the participants as to how the training will pay off on the job or for his/her career, or be otherwise rewarding. If this is not done, poorly focused or unrealistic programmes for change may lead to fuzzy results or failure. Employees can become discouraged by the slow pace of change or by the inertia of old habits. Trainers should help them use lapses and slip-ups as lessons to prepare themselves better for the future.

Lasting changes require sustained practice both on and off the job. A single seminar or workshop is just a beginning, but not sufficient in itself. Naturally arising opportunities for practice at work and at home should be used, and new behaviours practised repeatedly and consistently over a period of months. Change will be greater if the organisation's environment supports the change, values the competence and provides a safe environment for experimentation. When there is no real support, particularly from bosses, the change effort will seem hollow or too risky. Change that fits the values of the organisation should be encouraged. It should be demonstrated that competence is important for job placement, promotion, performance review, and so on.

Phase Three: Transfer and Maintenance

A particularly challenging aspect of social and emotional learning is the transfer and maintenance of learned skills. When learners return to their natural environment, there may still be many cues which support the old neural pathways that the training was designed to weaken. There may also be significant barriers to the use of some of the new social and emotional competencies that have a fragile neural foundation. Well-designed training programmes cannot be effective if the larger organisational system in which they are embedded is not supportive of the training goals. Recent research has identified several aspects of the organisational environment that can facilitate the transfer of emotional learning.

- **Encouraging the use of skills on the job** In many different ways supervisors, peers, subordinates and others in the work environment can encourage learners to apply what they have learned. The most effective ways of doing this include either reminding employees to apply the newly acquired skills or reinforcing them when they do so. Reinforcement is particularly effective in encouraging employees to apply their newly acquired skills on the job and in helping them to continue doing so.

    Reinforcement by a supervisor can be especially powerful at the workplace. Consider the following case. Participants of two training programmes enjoyed the sessions and successfully learned new skills. But follow-up assessment showed that the participants of the first programme actually applied their skills on the job, while those of the second did not. The difference between the two programmes was that the trainees in the first one were 'directed and encouraged by their supervisors to use the new skills'.

    Supervisors can reinforce the use of new skills on the job in subtle ways. For instance, they can encourage employees to apply learned skills on the job simply by cueing them to do so. Also, a follow-up assessment of skills acquired during training can make the trainees feel more accountable and increase transfer of learning. For example, airlines have 'check pilots' who observe flight crew during flights and give them feedback in order to encourage them to use teamwork, communication and leadership skills that they have learned.

The behaviour of a supervisor, or any person of high standing, is crucial to the transfer and maintenance of new emotional competencies. The models to which learners are exposed when they return to the work environment are even more powerful than those they encountered during training. Emotional behaviour is especially sensitive to the effects of modelling, and persons of high status serve as influential models in the workplace. For instance, in one supervisory training programme, participants were taught to adopt a more supportive leadership style. After they returned to their jobs, only those trainees whose own supervisors had transferred such a style to them were themselves able to bring it to their jobs.

In addition to modelling and reinforcement, reflection can also help transfer and maintain what has been learned. Supervisors can periodically allocate some time to help learners reflect on what they have done, apply the new skills, and review the barriers as well as facilitating factors. As self-awareness is the cornerstone of emotional competence, reflection can be particularly valuable during the transfer and maintenance phase.

Although supervisors play an important role in reinforcement and encouragement, other individuals and groups can also be just as important in the work environment. For instance, in a supervisory skills programme, employees were trained alongside the supervisors. This additional component of the programme helped create an environment that encouraged supervisors to practice and apply new behaviours.

- **Providing an organisational culture that supports learning**
  The transfer and maintenance of specific skills seems to be affected by the extent to which an organisation values learning and development in general. Challenging jobs, social

support, reward and development systems and an emphasis on innovation and competition influence such perceptions and expectations.

The work environment is particularly important for the transfer of social and emotional learning to the job. One study reported that participants of a human relations training programme who returned to a supportive climate performed better on objective performance measures and were promoted more often than those who worked in an unsupportive climate. These effects were not observed until 18 months after the training, highlighting the importance of a supportive environment for the development of social and emotional competencies over time.

Phase Four: Evaluating Change

- **Conducting ongoing evaluation research** Evaluation is essential in promoting effective training. Research reveals that many training programmes fail to fulfil their promises. It is only through evaluation that inadequate programmes be improved and effective ones retained. The term 'evaluation' refers to a process that focuses on continuous improvement rather than on just a 'pass–fail' test in which individuals associated with a programme win or lose credibility. When an evaluation indicates that a programme falls short in achieving its goals, it should not be used to punish an individual or a group. Rather, it should be used as a guide to improve the training that is offered. Evaluation should be linked to learning and the continuous pursuit of quality.

  Evaluation has attracted increasing attention of late because of the realisation that training departments in modern organisations need to be made more accountable. Instead of cost centres, training departments are now viewed as profit centres. Unfortunately, the concept of evaluating the effect of EQ training has not gained ground. A survey of 35 highly regarded companies conducted by the American Society for

Training and Development noted that of the 27 companies that attempted to promote emotional competence through training and development, more than two-thirds did not evaluate the effect of these efforts. Those that did relied primarily on measures such as reactions to training and employee opinion surveys. Adequate evaluations of social and emotional learning efforts have been rare. A major reason is the widespread belief that programmes designed to promote 'soft skills' cannot be evaluated. Although this may have once been true, it is no longer so because tools are now available to conduct rigorous evaluations of most training programmes designed to promote social and emotional competence.

As mentioned earlier, people of all ages can improve their social and emotional competence. However, the principles for developing this type of competence differ greatly from those that have guided much of the training and development practice in the past. Developing emotional competence calls for the unlearning of deeply ingrained habits of thought, feeling and action and the learning of new ones. Such a process requires motivation, effort, time, support and sustained practice. The guidelines discussed here highlight the importance of the Preparation and Transfer and Maintenance phases of the training process. Yet very often, in practice, these phases are neglected.

Organisations are increasingly providing training and development that are explicitly labeled as 'emotional intelligence' or 'emotional competence' training. The guidelines discussed here apply to any development effort in which personal and social learning is a goal. This would include most management and executive development efforts as well as training in supervisory skills, diversity, teamwork, leadership, conflict management, stress management, sales or customer relations.

Ideally, efforts to develop emotional competence should include all the elements identified here, but this may often not be feasible. Fortunately, the effects of adhering to the guidelines are multiple and synergistic: the more guidelines that trainers can follow, the greater and more lasting will be their impact.

If the current interest in promoting emotional intelligence at work is viewed as a sustained effort rather than just another management fad, it is important that practitioners follow the guidelines based on the best available research. Only when the training is based on sound, empirically tested methods can its promise be realised.

[Work Psychology and Human Resources Forum is an EQ Consulting firm and has helped with their inputs for this chapter. They can be contacted at CD-243, Vishakha Enclave, Pitam Pura, Delhi–110088. E-mail: wphrf2004@yahoo.com. Contact person Professor N.K. Chadha.]

7

Know Your EQ: Emotional Quotient Test

> There is nothing you can do angry that you can't do better when not angry.

The present EQ test is based on the operational definition proposed by Dalip Singh (2003) that 'emotional intelligence is the ability of an individual to appropriately and successfully respond to a vast variety of emotional stimuli being elicited from the inner self and immediate environment. Emotional intelligence constitutes three psychological dimensions, *emotional sensitivity*, *emotional maturity* and *emotional competency*, which motivate an individual to recognise truthfully, interpret honestly and handle tactfully the dynamics of human behavior'. The test has been designed in such a way that it measures all three dimensions.

Is it possible to measure these emotional dimensions? The answer is 'Yes'. This chapter includes an EQ test that will help measure one's emotional intelligence. This test has been standardised for professional managers, businessmen, bureaucrats, artists and graduate students. This EQ test has a test–retest and split–half *reliability* of 0.94 and 0.89 respectively and *validity* of 0.89. (To know more about making of this EQ test, refer to the Chapter 5 of this book).

The EQ Test

(Developed by Professor N.K. Chadha and Dr Dalip Singh)

Know your emotional quotient (EQ) How do you FEEL about yourself and people around you? This psychological test will help you to know more about yourself and about people around you. This test measures the way you use your emotional skills in your personal and professional life.

The 22 situations given below will measure your emotional responses to different situations. Answer on the basis of how you FEEL and not what you THINK. There are no right or wrong answers. Answer honestly and do not spend too much time. Usually your first response is the best response. Do not leave any question unanswered. You can also attempt the EQ Test online at www.eqindia.com.

Your Name: _____ Age: _____ Profession: _____
Gender: Male/Female. Qualifications: _____
Country: _____ Date: _____

Attempt the EQ Test Now

1. **You have been denied a promotion by the management for which you were eligible. Moreover, one of your juniors has been promoted. You are emotionally upset and feel frustrated. What will you do?**

    a. Talk it over with your boss and ask for reconsideration of the management's decision.
    b. Start abusing the colleague who superseded you.
    c. Move the court and obtain a stay order to get justice.
    d. Identify your shortcomings and try to improve your performance.

2. **A freshly recruited professional graduate joins your organisation as a management trainee. After a few weeks, she complains to you that she was not being taken seriously by her subordinates. What will you suggest her?**

    a. Ask her to handle the situation herself and not bother you with trivial matters.
    b. Tell her that such behaviour should be ignored.

c. Ask her to be bold, face the challenge and overcome the problem.
   d. Empathise with her and help her figure out ways to get others to work with her.

3. **At the workplace, due to some misunderstanding, your colleagues stop talking to you. You are convinced that there was no fault of yours. How will you react?**
   a. Wait till they come and start talking to you again.
   b. Take the initiative, go forward and start talking to them.
   c. Let things take their own time to improve.
   d. Ask someone to mediate.

4. **You get into an argument with your colleague and end up attacking him/her personally. Later you realise that you never intended to tarnish the image of your colleague. How will you handle such an ugly situation?**
   a. Sit calmly and consider what triggered off the arguments, and if it was possible to control your anger at that point of time.
   b. Avoid future arguments and leave the room.
   c. Apologise to your colleague for your behaviour.
   d. Continue with the argument till you reach some definite conclusion.

5. **Imagine you are an insurance salesperson selling insurance policies. You approach a number of prospective clients who slam the door on your face and refuse to buy policies. What will you do?**
   a. Blame yourself and stop work for the day.
   b. Reassess your capabilities as an insurance salesperson.
   c. Come out with fresh strategies to overcome similar situations in future.
   d. Contact the clients again some other day.

6. **When someone directly criticises your behaviour, how will you behave?**
   a. Tend to close up and stop listening.
   b. Carefully listen to their opinion.

c. Tend to get upset about it.
   d. Think of ways to change your behaviour.

7. **You are on an aircraft and suddenly the air hostess announces that it has been hijacked by the terrorists. Everyone is in a state of shock. What will be your reaction?**

   a. Blame yourself for choosing an inauspicious day for travelling.
   b. Be in emotional control and attend to the instructions of the pilot/air hostess.
   c. Continue to read your magazine and pay little attention to the incident.
   d. Cry out and vow not to travel by air in future.

8. **Imagine you are a police officer posted in a sensitive area. You get information of violent ethnic clashes between two religious communities in which people have been killed from both sides and property damaged. What action will you take?**

   a. Decide not to visit the spot personally as there may be a danger to your life.
   b. Relax; this is not the first time riots have taken place.
   c. Try to handle the situation by taking action according to the law.
   d. Reach the spot and assuage the feelings of the victims.

9. **Your grown up daughter starts arguing with you every now and then. She tells you that you cannot impose your old-fashioned attitudes and outdated values on her. How will you tackle her?**

   a. Accept her statement in helplessness and take a low-profile position in the family.
   b. Send her to a psychologist to learn how to adjust with her environment.
   c. Manage your emotions and explain your point of view as patiently as possible.
   d. Talk to her and understand her emotions, beliefs and attitudes.

10. After weeks of merger of two largest financial firms, hundreds of employees were expected to lose their jobs. You, being the General Manager (HQ), were told to convey to the employee the decision of the management. How will you convey the message?

   a. Give a gloomy picture and tell them you have no option but to fire half of them.
   b. Give a bright picture and tell them that the company will be blessed with talented people from both firms.
   c. Tell them that you will collect more information to be fair and update them every few days on how things will take shape.
   d. Announce the decision and let the employees take a decision about what they want.

11. You are a professor in a college. While delivering a lecture, a student comments that you have not prepared the topic properly and you are just passing the time. This has hurt your self-esteem. What will be your reaction?

   a. Report to the principal of the college about the unruly behaviour of the student.
   b. Order the student to leave the classroom at once.
   c. Ask him/her to meet you in your chamber after the class to explain what he/she wants.
   d. Judge the emotions of the class and promise to make amendments accordingly.

12. As CEO of a company, during a meeting with the union, one of the union leaders levels serious allegations of corruption and favouritism against you. How will you react?

   a. Continue with the discussion and listen to their demands with a cool head.
   b. Ask the union leader to make allegations in writing and offer an impartial enquiry.
   c. Cancel further negotiation and ask the union leader to apologise first.

d. Leave the room after assigning the responsibility to your subordinate to continue with the meeting.

13. **You had an argument with your spouse on some trivial family matter and are not on speaking terms for some time. The situation is causing mental disturbance to both of you. What will you do?**

    a. Stick to your stand; after all you were never at fault.
    b. Try to break the ice by analysing the reasons for the conflict.
    c. Make the first move and ease the situation.
    d. Wait for your spouse to make the first move to restore normalcy.

14. **You hail from a rural area and take admission in a city college. You find your classmates taunting you as you are not smart and are unable to speak good English. How will you manage yourself?**

    a. Ignore them.
    b. Shout back and tell them to mind their own business.
    c. Leave studies half way and go back to your village.
    d. Accept their challenge and prove that you can match them.

15. **While speaking to an audience, you feel that:**

    a. It is difficult to convey your speech.
    b. You are partially comfortable in conveying your speech.
    c. You are comfortable in conveying your speech.
    d. You feel that you will do better with some more practice.

16. **Your friend's sister, who got married just one year back, is heading for a divorce. She is highly educated and economically self-dependent. She comes to you for guidance. What will you advise her?**

    a. Tell her to go ahead with the divorce as she is a first class MBA and her husband cannot take her for granted.
    b. Empathise with her for marrying an academically average person.

c. Advise her to talk to her husband and figure out the reasons behind the maladjustment.
d. Tell her that academic qualifications are important but these do not help in leading a successful married life.

17. **There is a blind girl in your class. She trips on her way out of the class. You see a few of your friends making fun of her and laughing at her. What will you do?**

    a. Laugh along with your friends.
    b. Ignore the incident, as they are your friends.
    c. Help the blind girl make her way out of the classroom but say nothing to your friends.
    d. Help the girl and then confront your friends for being so insensitive.

18. **While having an argument with someone, if you lose, you:**

    a. Feel totally beaten.
    b. Wait for the next opportunity to beat your opponents.
    c. Winning and losing are part of the game.
    d. Analyse the reasons for the loss.

19. **You are working as HRD General Manager in a large multinational company which recruits dozens of fresh MBAs, engineers and other professionals in senior positions every year. This requires time, energy and money. However, you find that 75 per cent of the young recruits are leaving the company after around two years of work experience to join more attractive jobs. What will you do?**

    a. Ignore the trend. There is rampant unemployment and you can find more people lined up to join your company.
    b. Try to find out the root cause of their leaving the job and take corrective measures to retain them as you have already invested heavily in them.
    c. Increase the pay package and lure them in working with you.
    d. Change the selection criteria and recruit people on the basis of their need and requirements.

20. You have been involuntarily transferred to a remote project and posted under a new boss. Although you have been given a pay hike and also a promise for promotion in the near future, yet you are not comfortable. Your family cannot shift along with you due to education of your children. You are in a sensitive area and your security is also at risk. You are undergoing a mild level of stress. How will you diffuse the stress?

   a. Enjoy. After all there has been a hike in your pay for working in a sensitive area.
   b. Wait. It may turn out to be an opportunity for early promotion.
   c. Lament. Why should such terrible things happen to only you?
   d. Act in haste. Think of resigning and find a new job for yourself.

21. You have lived your life for so many years on this earth. How would you like to explain your life at the moment in one sentence?

   a. Successful: Well, I am a contended person who has got whatever could make me feel happy.
   b. OK: Well, it's a mixed experience for me. It's 50:50.
   c. Comfortable: Well, destiny is in the hands of God. Man is just a puppet.
   d. Uncomfortable: Well, I feel I deserved better but could not get it.

22. As an HRD manager, you have to recruit a large number of employees for a multinational firm. After the written test and interview you find that most of candidates who qualified are women. What will be your reaction?

   a. Hire women employees. They deserve it as they have qualified the selection criteria.
   b. Well it's a women's world. Hire them any way.
   c. Hire male and female employees in equal number.
   d. Avoid women employees as they are a liability.

Your Answer Sheet

1. a	9. a	17. a
b	b	b
c	c	c
d	d	d
2. a	10. a	18. a
b	b	b
c	c	c
d	d	d
3. a	11. a	19. a
b	b	b
c	c	c
d	d	d
4. a	12. a	20. a
b	b	b
c	c	c
d	d	d
5. a	13. a	21. a
b	b	b
c	c	c
d	d	d
6. a	14. a	22. a
b	b	b
c	c	c
d	d	d
7. a	15. a	
b	b	
c	c	
d	d	
8. a	16. a	
b	b	
c	c	
d	d	

Calculate Your Score by Using This Scoring Key

Q. No.	Response	Score	Q. No.	Response	Score
1.	a	15	12.	a	20
	b	5		b	15
	c	10		c	10
	d	20		d	5
2.	a	5	13.	a	5
	b	10		b	15
	c	15		c	20
	d	20		d	10
3.	a	15	14.	a	10
	b	20		b	15
	c	5		c	5
	d	10		d	20
4.	a	20	15.	a	10
	b	15		b	15
	c	10		c	20
	d	5		d	5
5.	a	5	16.	a	5
	b	20		b	10
	c	15		c	15
	d	10		d	20
6.	a	10	17.	a	5
	b	20		b	10
	c	5		c	15
	d	15		d	20
7.	a	5	18.	a	5
	b	20		b	10
	c	15		c	15
	d	10		d	20
8.	a	10	19.	a	5
	b	5		b	20
	c	20		c	15
	d	15		d	10
9.	a	5	20.	a	15
	b	10		b	20
	c	20		c	10
	d	15		d	5

Contd.

Contd.

Q. No.	Response	Score	Q. No.	Response	Score
10.	a	5	21.	a	20
	b	20		b	15
	c	15		c	10
	d	10		d	5
11.	a	5	22.	a	20
	b	10		b	15
	c	15		c	10
	d	20		d	5

Quantitative Analysis of Your Scores

EQ Dimensions	Situations	Your Score	Your P (percentile)
SENSITIVITY	2-8-16-17-22 (5 situations)	——	——
MATURITY	4-6-9-11-12-18-21 (7 situations)	——	——
COMPETENCY	1-3-5-7-10-13-14-15-19-20 (10 situations)	——	——
TOTAL EQ SCORE	All Situations (22 situations)	——	——

The Percentile Table

EQ Dimensions	P-90	P-75	P-50	P-40	P-20
SENSITIVITY (Range of score: 25–100)	93–100	86–92	66–85	36–65	< 35
MATURITY (Range of Score: 35–140)	133–140	113–132	88–112	53–87	< 52
COMPETENCY (Range of score: 50–200)	168–200	141–168	97–140	71–96	< 70
TOTAL EQ	379–440	308–379	261–307	159–260	< 158

Qualitative Analysis of Your Scores

Percentile	Interpretation
P-90	Extremely high EQ
P-75	High EQ
P-50	Moderate EQ
P-40	Low EQ
P-20	Try the test again some other day.

MODEL EQ GRAPHS OF VARIOUS PROFESSIONS

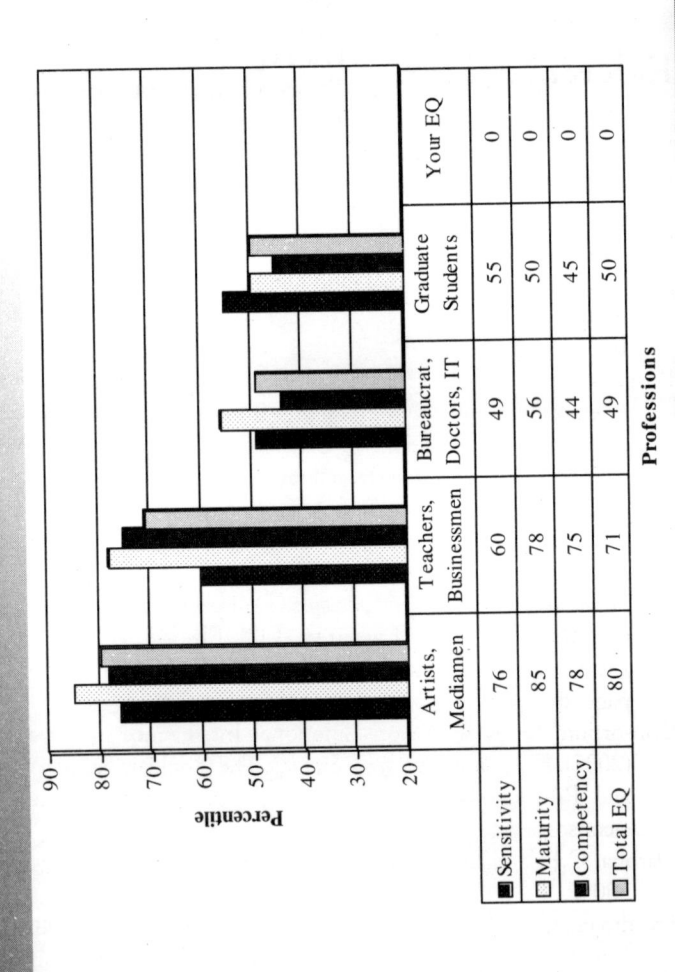

	Artists, Mediamen	Teachers, Businessmen	Bureaucrat, Doctors, IT	Graduate Students	Your EQ
■ Sensitivity	76	60	49	55	0
□ Maturity	85	78	56	50	0
■ Competency	78	75	44	45	0
□ Total EQ	80	71	49	50	0

Professions

References and Select Bibliography

Bangar, Ravi (2005). Presidential address delivered at the Indo–Singapore Chamber of Commerce and Industry, Singapore, 24 December 2005.

Bar-On, R. (1997). 'Emotional Quotient Inventory (EQ-i): Multi-Health Systems', *Technical Manual*. Toronto, Canada: Multi-health Systems Inc.

Boyatzis, R., D. Goleman and K. Rhee (2000). 'Clustering competence in emotional intelligence: Insights from the emotional competence inventory (ECI)'. In R. Bar-On and J.D.A. Parker (eds), *Handbook of Emotional Intelligence*. San Francisco: Jossey-Bass.

Chabungbam, Parmananda (2005). 'The Soft Art of Being a Tough Leader', *India Management Journal*, pp. 82–84, November 2005.

Chadha, Narender K. (2005). *Human Resource Management Issues: Case Studies and Experimental Execises*. Delhi: Shri Sai Printographers.

Cooper, Robert (1996). Executive EQ: Emotional Intelligence in Leadership and Organizations, New York: Berkley Publication Group, page xiii.

Consortium for Research on Emotional Intelligence in Organisations (2005). *Emotional Intelligence Services*. The Graduate School of Applied and Professional Psychology, Rutgers University. Website: www.eiconsortium.org/.

Darolia, C.R. and Darolia, Shashi (2005): *The Punjab Heritage*, vol. 20, 2005.

Freedman, J., A. Jenson, M. Rideout and P. Freedman (1998). *Handle With Care: Emotional Intelligence Activity Book*. California: Six Seconds Publication.

Gardner, Howard (1993). *Frames of Mind: The Theory of Multiple Intelligences* (10th Anniversary Edition). New York: Basic Books.

Goleman, Daniel (1996). *Emotional Intelligence: Why It can Matter More than IQ*. New York: Bantam Books.

Goleman, Daniel (1998). *Working with Emotional Intelligence*. New York: Bantam Books.

Kapadia, Mala (2004). *Emotional Intelligence: A Workbook for Beginners*. New Delhi: BPI (India) Private Ltd.

Malekar, Samira (2005). 'Managing Human Capital: An EQ Perspective'. Unpublished paper presented at the National Conference at Institute of Technology and Management, Kharagpur, Navi Mumbai, India, 7–9 December 2005.

Mohan, Jitendra (2003). 'Emotional Intelligence Questionnaire', *Training Instrument*. Chandigarh, India: Panjab University.

Punia, B.K. (2005): 'Impact of Demographic Variables on Emotional Intelligence and Leadership Behaviour of Corporate Executives', *Journal of Organisational Behaviour*, IV(2), April, 2005, pp. 7–22.

Rajkhowa, Roopsmita (2002). *Emotional Intelligence of IAS Officers*. Unpublished work carried out in the Department of Psychology, University of Delhi, India.

Salovey, Peter and John Mayer (1990). 'Emotional Intelligence', *Imagination, Cognition and Personality*, Vol. 9, pp. 185–211.

——— (1997). 'What Is Emotional Intelligence?'. In P. Salovey and D.J. Sluyter (eds), *Emotional Development and Emotional Intelligence*. Basic Books: New York.

Sanwal, Vinod (2004). *Emotional Intelligence: The Indian Scenario*. New Delhi: Indian Publisher Distributers.

Sehgal, Meena (1999). 'A Study of EQ, Intelligence, Personality and Psychological Well Being of Adolescents'. *Asian Journal of Psychology and Education*, 32(1–2): 17–19.

Seligman, Martin (1995). *Explanatory Styles*. Hillsdale: Lawrence Erlbaum.

Singh, Dalip (2003). *Emotional Intelligence at Work: A Professional Guide*, 2nd edition, New Delhi: Sage Publications.

——— (2003). 'Do Different Professions Require Different Levels of Emotional Intelligence?', *International Journal of Behavioural Sciences*, 20(12), pp. 21–29.

——— (2005). 'EQ and Managerial Effectiveness: An International Study'. D. Litt. thesis, Bundelkhand University, Jhansi, India.

Sitaram, Lakshmi (2005): 'Relationship between EQ and IQ among Adolescents'. Unpublished Ph.D. work submitted to University of Bangalore, India.

Thorndike, E.L. (1920). 'Intelligence and its Uses', *Harper's Magazine*, Vol. 140, pp. 227–35.
Wechsler, D. (1940). 'Non-intellective Factors in General Intelligence', *Psychological Bulletin*, Vol. 37, pp. 444–45.
Yate, Martin (1977). *Career Smarts, Jobs with a Future.* New York: Ballantine Books.

Index

abhorrence, 31
ability, abilities, 20–22, 43, 45, 50, 59, 60, 74, 84, 95, 104, 117, 120–21, 128–29, 131, 168, 192, 210; deficiency, 26; emotional (non-intellective), 105; intellective, 105; social, 27
absenteeism, 64, 85, 91, 169
academic achievements, intelligence, 19–20, 22, 27, 29, 35, 37, 38, 57, 60, 65, 107, 216; and success, 19–22, 52, 69, 83, 105, 164; *see also* workplace
acceptance, 31, 80
accomplishment, 22, 42, 79, 177
accountability, 30, 64, 120
achievement drive, 160
achievement orientation, 47, 118, 152, 178
acrimony, 31
actions, 30, 52, 56, 166; and emotions/feelings, 58, 112, 194, 201, 208
adaptability, 22, 42, 111–12, 118, 129, 195
adeptness, 131
adjustment, 153; emotional intelligence and intelligence, relationship, 154–55; social, 104
adolescence, 49, 61; emotional quotient and IQ relations, 152–55, 187; emotional quotient and well-being, 165–68

adoration, 31
adulthood, 61
adults, emotional intelligence, 61, 193
affection, 19, 92
affinity, 31
age: and emotional intelligence, 61, 145; impact on emotional intelligence and leadership behaviour, 147–49; and managerial effectiveness, 165; mental and chronological, 50–51
alcoholism and drug abuse, 64, 81, 85, 87, 97, 99
aloofness, 31
altruism, 187
amazement, 32
American Management Association, 88
American Society for Training and Development, 208
amusement, 31
amygdala, 54
analysing, 37, 42, 178
anger, aggression, 19, 23, 31, 32, 38, 40, 51, 54, 55, 64, 67, 72, 75–77, 85, 87, 97, 109, 111, 141, 169, 189, 203; control/management, 96–102, 174–75
animosity, 31
annoyance, 31
anxiety, 31, 38, 40, 55, 72, 81, 85, 90, 92, 95, 97, 101, 109, 112, 161, 166, 169, 189

appreciation, 78, 92
apprehension, 31, 54
arousal, 54, 112, 128
assertion, assertiveness, 72, 108
astonishment, 31
attitudes, *see* beliefs and attitudes
attrition, 69, 169
attunement, 79, 95
authenticity, 190
authoritarianism, 48, 145
aversion, 31
awareness, 36, 45; emotional, 74, 131–32; organisational, 118–19; social, 115, 118–19; *see also* self-awareness

balance, 26, 56, 75, 166; *see also* heart and mind
Bar-On Emotional Quotient Inventory (EQ-I), 35, 108
Bar-On, Reuven, 168
behaviour, 36, 42, 45, 53, 60, 71–72, 78, 88, 95, 100, 107, 109, 121, 124, 168, 176, 178, 189, 193, 198, 206, 210, 212; change, 34, 202–3, 213; compulsive, 97; coping, 103; pattern, 110–12; stress symptoms, 85, 87
beliefs and attitudes, 30, 104, 178, 213; dysfunctional, 81; negative, 100
belongingness, 136, 161
bias, 147–49
bitterness, 96, 113
bliss, 31
body language, 188
body, *see* mind and body
boredom, 32, 85, 90
brain, 24, 51, 53, 54, 65, 107, 130, 145, 188, 189, 194; analytical capability, 75
building bonds, 120
burnout, 38, 40, 109, 138, 161, 170
business orientation, 178

business, benefits of emotional quotient (EQ), 48, 79, 189–91

capabilities, 168; and demands, mismatch, 169–70
cerebral simulation, 60
certainty, 32, 74
Chadha, N.K., 36, 124, 133, 142, 147, 179, 186
change, change process, 74, 91, 120, 153, 201–5; adaptation, 42; evaluation, 207–9; handling/ management, 187; positive, 78; preparation for, 194–99; recognising readiness to, 198–99, 204; resistance, 148; self directed, 200
cheerlessness, 31
children, childhood, 29, 38–39, 60–61; delayed gratification 24–26; emotional development, 60; *see also* school, benefits of emotional quotient
clarity, emotional, 106; of thinking, 43
coalition building, 119
Coca-Cola Corporation, 67–68
cognition, cognitive capacities, intelligence, 35, 36, 103, 107, 190; learning, 193
cohesion, 101, 152
collaboration, 83, 120–21, 188; *see also* teamwork
commitment, 79, 90, 101, 121, 197
commonsense, 84; practicality, 78
communication, 36, 62, 67, 89, 91, 96, 105, 116, 119, 128, 156, 176, 178, 186; non-verbal, 43, 113, 137; verbal, 22, 113
comparing, 37
compassion, 55, 56, 66, 98, 99, 102
competition, competitiveness, 43, 163
competitive advantage, 27
complacence, 32

concentration, 51, 85
concepts and ideas formation, 52
confidence, 22, 81, 110, 112, 152, 166, 169, 194
conflict(s), 71, 88–90, 101, 128, 138, 145, 198; avoidance, 66, 88, 141; individual, 88–89; management/handling, 81, 88, 116, 119, 209; resolution, 42–43, 88, 89, 91, 152, 181
conformity, 72
connections, 193–94
conscientiousness, 116, 117–18
Consortium for Research on Emotional Intelligence in Organisations (2000), 158; (2005), 66, 108, 115, 123, 192
contempt, 31
contentment, 31, 92, 177
cooperation, 22, 101, 131
coordination, 62, 64, 163
coping strategies, 103, 168, 174–75
corporate culture, 101
corruption, 64
courage, 31, 32, 39
creativity, 22, 35, 43, 66, 83, 138, 190
credibility, 62
criticism, 34, 78
cues: emotional, 128, 137; non-verbal, 77, 118
cultural diversity, 147
culture of sharing, 161
customer relations, satisfaction, service, 48, 67–68, 74, 84, 91, 101, 107, 118, 189, 192, 209

decision-making, 42, 43, 54, 137
defeatism, 46
defensiveness, 102, 197, 201
deficiency, 94
dejection, 31
delayed gratification, 25, 58, 99, 111, 128, 189

delight, 31
demographic factors, 154, 156
depression, 31, 46, 72, 85, 97, 140, 166, 187, 189
desires, 25, 52
despair, 31, 38
developing others, 111, 119
devotion, 31
disappointment, 38, 92
disdain, 31
disgust, 19, 31, 54
distaste, 31
distress, 49, 60, 169
distrust, 19, 64
diversity, 146–48, 151, 209
doubt, 32
drug abuse, *see* alcoholism

ecstasy, 31
effectiveness, 21, 111, 119, 151, 169, 178, 196; organisational, 146, 176; leadership, 145–46, 152; managerial and emotional quotient, 155–65; of training, 204
efficacy, 81
efficiency, 195
egoism, ego, 23, 110, 128
embarrassment, 31, 54
emotion inventory, 180, 182
emotional abuse, 99
emotional balance, 88
emotional bonding, 121, 162
emotional capabilities, 21
emotional competencies, 21–22, 27, 29, 36–38, 61, 63, 64, 69–71, 73–74, 76, 81, 90, 101, 108, 109–10, 115–16, 123, 127–28, 131–32, 134, 138–39, 159, 168, 177–78, 192–94, 197, 202, 210; requirements, 177; training, 190, 195–96, 200–8
emotional development, 60, 192*ff*
emotional disorders, 97

emotional disturbances, 29
emotional education, 60
emotional environment, 121
emotional intelligence (EI)/
    emotional quotient (EQ), 19–27,
    29–37, 39, 42–46, 48, 57, 60, 61,
    64, 73, 74, 79–80, 91, 98, 103,
    166; competencies, 115–21;
    defining, 104–13; how to acquire,
    37–41; development, examples,
    66–72; develops with maturity,
    61–64; defining, 122–23; five
    attributes, 176; gender specific,
    49; Indian context, 156; in
    Indian perspective, 121–30;
    and intelligence quotient (IQ),
    relationship, 50ff; levels required
    for various jobs, 113–15, 130–45;
    low and high, consequences,
    55–58; makes difference in life,
    26–29; application in
    organisations, 42–45, 62, 66–72;
    non-cognitive, 51; helps in
    professional success, 41–48;
    some myths about, 48–49;
    and work performance, 62–64
emotional quotient test, 63, 109,
    124–27, 133–35, 142–45, 157,
    168, 179–87, 210ff; B-coefficient
    technique, 136; item analysis,
    181–85;—chi-square, 183–85;
    —skewness, 182–83; non-
    probability sampling technique,
    134, 142–45; reliability, 185;
    situation selection, 180–81;
    validity, 185–86
emotional literacy, 102
emotional management, *see* emotions,
    management/control
emotional reaction, 50, 54, 66, 77,
    94, 203
emotional stability, 147–49, 151–52
emotional stimuli, 36, 109, 124, 127,
    129, 210

emotional upsets, 36, 52, 75, 109,
    211; management, 84–92
emotional winner, 75, 92–94;
    vs loser, 94–95
emotions, 19, 23–24, 27, 30–32, 35,
    36, 39–40, 42, 49, 51–54, 56–58,
    59, 60–61, 63, 65, 71–72, 74,
    80, 83, 84, 90, 95–96, 100, 102,
    106–7, 111–12, 118, 128,
    130–31, 155, 158, 188–89, 213;
    communicable, 113;
    management/control, 58, 75,
    84–92, 106–7, 119, 138, 152,
    160, 166, 170, 174, 175, 187;
    positive or negative, 54–55, 86,
    101, 109, 113, 128, 160, 169;
    and rational intelligence, 50;
    recognition, 75–77; can be
    unlearned, 64–66
empathy, 21, 27, 36, 46, 49, 56, 57,
    61, 64, 70, 74, 75, 77–80, 98,
    100, 108, 112, 114, 118, 131,
    132–33, 138, 152, 170, 175,
    176–78, 189, 215
employee(s), 44, 85, 91, 197;
    commitment, 79, 90, 99, 101,
    121, 203; and employer, relation
    between, 161; identify strength
    and weaknesses, 78–79;
    motivation, 96, 177;
    pre-employment screening
    process, 68–69; self-esteem, 81;
    see also workplace
encouragement, 43, 197–98, 205–7
enmity, 54
enthusiasm, 140
environment, 44
equanimity, 32
euphoria, 31
Europe: management practices, 156,
    158–60, 162–65
evaluation, 207–9
exasperation, 31
excellence, 204

excitement, 30
expectations, 198
experience, 24, 53, 61, 69, 75, 78, 98, 160, 194; and managerial effectiveness, 164
experimentation, experimental methods of emotional learning, 201–2, 205
extroversion, 104, 129; and EQ, positive correlation, 168
Eysenck, Hans, 129; personality dimension, 167–68

failures, 20, 46–48, 69, 81, 83, 91, 99, 204; emotional, 145
fait accompli, 54
faith, 32
family bonding, relationships, 37, 71, 99, 104, 121–22, 153, 154, 161; impact of stress, 87
fear, fears, 31, 32, 51, 53, 54, 72, 81, 87, 109, 140
feedback, 26, 46, 72, 90–91, 101, 117, 169, 196–97, 201, 203; negative, 110, 170
feelings, 23, 30, 33, 35, 42, 52, 56, 71, 80–81, 84, 101–2, 103, 111, 116–17, 124, 146, 157, 174, 196, 203; and actions, relationship, 112, 194, 201, 208; negative, 64; positive, 97
flexibility, 66, 108, 170
focus, 170, 188
focus group discussions, 63, 90
forgiveness, 32
friendliness, 31, 33, 64, 77
frustration, 36, 38, 40, 46, 60, 62, 67, 83, 92, 99, 100, 109, 128, 140, 156, 161, 169, 170, 187, 189, 211

gender, 153, 156, 158; impact on emotional intelligence and leadership behaviour, 150–51

genetic factors, 129–30
gestures, 78, 137, 162
goals and objectives, 25, 48, 52, 101, 107, 120, 129, 152, 156, 157, 166, 177, 198, 200; breaking into manageable steps, 200
Goleman, Daniel, 106–8, 130, 133, 167, 168, 176, 186
Graham, Lawrence Otis, 146
gratification, 31
grief, 31, 72
grouchiness, 98
group discussions, 201
guilt, 31, 99

habits, 38, 46, 73, 194, 204, 208
happiness, 31, 45, 55, 56, 60, 71, 92, 131, 166
harmony, 138, 162
hate, 55
head and heart, dichotomy, 37, 39, 50
health, health problems, 57, 71; anger-related, 97, 100–2; stress related, 85–86, 169; at workplace, 85, 88, 187
heart, 145, 146; and mind balance, 128; software powers, 24; triumph over head, 50
helplessness, 94
honesty, 190
hope, 32
hostility, 31, 46, 171, 188
human resource management, 168, 193; EQ perspective, 176–79
humiliation, 31, 141
humour, 169, 187
hurt, 38, 76–77, 97, 98, 141
hyperactivity, 72

IAS Officers emotional intelligence, 139–45
immune system, 101
impatience, 98
impersonal relations, 121

impulse control, 58, 137, 166, 169
impulsiveness, 129, 131, 174
income and managerial effectiveness, 165
indignation, 31
infatuation, 31
inferiority complex, 109–10
influence, influencing, 75, 95–96, 116, 119, 178
information age, 60
initiative, 21, 27, 70, 83, 118, 140
inner self, *see* self
inner voice, 81
innovative culture, thinking, 43, 176
insecurity, 101, 140, 166
insight enhancing, 203
insurance sector, and emotional quotient (EQ), 45–46, 70, 82–84, 137, 195
integrity, 190
intelligence, intellect, 19, 21, 26, 42, 50, 103, 116, 130, 167, 169; cognitive 51; and non-cognitive, 153
intelligence quotient (IQ), 19–21, 23, 25–27, 29–30, 33–35, 43, 61, 108; and emotional quotient (EQ), relationship, 50*ff*, 166, 168; test, 50–51
intentions, 117
interaction, 114, 196
interdependence, 152
inter-personal: conflicts, 39, 161; confluence, 36; effectiveness, 22; relations, *see* relationships
interpretation and perception, 30
introspection, 94
introversion, 104, 129
irritability, 31, 67, 85, 90, 98, 99
isolation, 65

Japan, management practices, 156, 158–59, 161–65
jealousy, 32, 55

job dissatisfaction, 40, 85, 90
job performance, *see* performance at workplace
job satisfaction, 40, 47, 136
job security, 21
joy, 55, 57

kindness, 31, 77
knowledge, 37–38, 163; emotional, 35; social, 104

leader(s), leadership, leadership behaviour, 21, 22–23, 57, 62, 70, 102, 156, 176, 178, 187, 190, 206, 209; development, 146; emotional intelligence and, 145–47; effectiveness, 145–46, 152; impact of age, 147–49; impact of gender, 150–51; impact of marital status, 149; orientation, 146; visionary, 119–20, 131
learning, learning process, 47, 57, 65–66, 73, 77, 81, 117, 131, 188, 207; cognitive and technical, 193; emotional, 160, 193–94, 196–203, 205; experiences, 37; goals linking to personal values, 198; social, 37, 202, 205, 208
learning organisations, emotional intelligence, 146–47
lecture method, 201
limbic system, 54
listening and observation, 43, 78, 200
loneliness, 31, 140
love, 31, 77
lust, 54

Macaulay's report, 1854, 140
maladjustment, 63; at workplace, 131
Malekar, Shamira, 176
management, manager, 32, 63, 66, 78, 91, 96, 122, 177, 197, 201; and conflict resolution, 89; and

emotional intelligence, 85–86, 155–65; should learn emotional skills, 73*ff*; of human capital an EQ perspective, 176–79; Indian style, 122–27; poor, 145, un-empathetic, 80
mania, 31
manipulation, 32, 64
marital status, impact on emotional intelligence and leadership behaviour, 147, 149
Marshmallow experiment, 24–25
Mastery, 61, 200
maturity, 61–64; emotional, 36, 63, 110–12, 128, 210
memory, 43, 72, 103, 188; emotional, 54
mental health, 168, 187
Meyerson, Mort, 67
mind, 30, 36, 43, 51–52, 146; and body, 146, 169; emotional and rational, 53–54
Mischel, Walter, 24–25
misunderstanding, 212
modelling, 202, 206
mood(s), 49, 52, 75, 103, 106, 128, 131; management, 166; swings, 169
morale, 46, 63, 64
mortification, 31
motivation, 21, 22–23, 35, 36, 46, 52, 61, 63, 66, 74, 78, 92, 101, 102, 105, 129, 131, 152, 156, 164, 166, 169, 176–78, 181, 194–95, 198, 199, 200, 208

needs assessment, 195, 204
negativities, negative dimensions, 78, 166
neo-cortex, 54
nervousness, 31
networking, 119, 120
neural connections, 194, 201, 203, 205

neuroticism psychoticism and EQ, negative correlation, 168
non-cognition, 103
non-emotional aspects, 103
nurturing attitude, 152

occupational health, *see* health at workplace
on-the-job capabilities, 74
openness, 119
optimism, 36, 45, 46, 57, 66, 69, 71, 83, 108, 110, 118, 128, 166, 170, 187, 189
organisation(s), organisational, 42, 44–45, 176–78, 204–8; behaviour and culture, 69, 90, 120, 193; effectiveness, 146, 176; emotional intelligence, 62, 66–70, 84; and employees' self-esteem, 81; goals, 164; need assessment, 195, 204; stress, 87, 169; *see also* management, training and development
overwork, 85, 149

pain, 55, 86
panic, 31
paranoia, 87
participation, 197–98
passion, 23, 30
patience, 151, 174
peace, 55, 92
people skills, 166
performance, 68–69, 70, 92, 97, 121, 141, 152, 154, 176, 202, 205; appraisal, 179; and emotional intelligence, 169–70; feedback, 23, 87; impact of stress, 86, 87, 168–70; individual and organisational, 88; theory, 108, 129; at work place, 38, 62, 84, 99, 116–18, 131, 195; *see also* job-satisfaction, success, workplace
perseverance, 84, 95

persistence, 129
personal: effectiveness, 178; evaluation, 166; issues and work, 67; management, 22; satisfaction, 44; worth, 81
personality, 21, 55, 87, 96, 121; characteristics, 32–33, 83; development, 38, 52, 105; dimensions, 167; disorganised, 100; and emotional experiences, 168; traits, 38, 112, 129–30, 168
personality theory, 107–8, 129–30
perturbation, 30
pessimism, 46, 94, 187
PHD chamber of commerce and industry (PHDCCI), New Delhi, interactive workshop, 123–27
phobia, 31
pity, 31
planning, 178
powerlessness, 99
practice, 72; and learning, relationship, 201, 208
pride, 31, 129
problem solving, 42, 97, 103, 137
procrastination, 85
productivity, 21, 40, 63, 70, 71, 84, 85, 99, 101, 145
professional success, role of emotional quotient (EQ), 41–48
professions/jobs, different require different emotional quotient (EQ), 113–15, 130–45
promotions, 45, 57
psychological, psychology: characteristics, 123–24; coaching, 90–91; dimensions of emotional intelligence, 109, 129; factors, 134; maladjustments, 63; and management, 201; needs, 100; test, 51; well being, 166–68

qualification and managerial effectiveness, 164

quality, 44, 165
qualm, 31

rage, 77
rationality, rational intelligence, 50, 53–54, 100, 170
reason, reasoning, 25, 52–53; and emotion dichotomy, 50, 56, 106, 130, 157, 188
reflection, 206
regret, 31, 77
rehearsal and emotional inhibition, 174
reinforcement, 205–6
relapse prevention, 203–4
relationships, inter-personal relations, 29, 34, 36–38, 57, 62, 64, 71, 80, 88, 100, 104, 108, 110–12, 128, 155–56; forge, 193; management, 115–16, 119–21, 175, 181
relaxation, 200
remorse, 31
repetition, 201
resentment, 31, 97, 99
resilience, 25, 66, 101, 170, 190, 195
resourcefulness, 19
respect, mutual respect, 64, 81, 91, 101, 138, 197
response, creative, 22; emotional, 53, 64, 196
retrenchments, 162
revulsion, 31
rigidity, 90, 97
risk avoidance, 160
role models, 37
role play, 201
rustout, 170

sadness, 19, 31, 32, 54, 72
salesmanship, emotional intelligence, 82–84
satisfaction, 22, 23, 31, 44, 88, 115, 166, 176; *see also* job satisfaction
scepticism, 195

school, benefits of emotional quotient, 188–89
scorn, 31, 38
security, 161
self, 23, 55, 109–11, 210
self-acceptance, 166
self-assessment, 90, 117
self-awareness, 74, 107–8, 111, 115, 116, 131–32, 166, 170, 181, 195, 203, 206
self-confidence, 49, 70, 74, 84, 117, 138, 152, 194, 196, 200
self-control, 24, 25, 46, 90, 120, 128, 192
self-dependence, 152
self-discipline, 46, 114, 117, 131
self-efficacy, 200
self-esteem, 36, 39, 56, 71, 75, 80–84, 99, 109, 110, 128, 165, 166, 196, 199
self-improvement, 176
self-interest, 110
self-management, 107, 115, 116, 187, 191, 195
self-pity, 31
self-regulation, 62, 74, 131, 166, 170, 181
self-reliance, 39
self-righteousness, 81, 97
senses, 54
sensitivity, 197; emotional, 36, 63, 72, 112–15, 128, 210
service, 118
shame, 19, 31, 99
shared responsibility, 152
shareholder satisfaction, 44
shock, 31
shyness, 65
simulations, 201
skills, 42, 113, 119, 168, 178, 203, 205; emotional, 23, 44–45, 64, 65, 69, 72, 78, 91, 97, 111, 130, 137, 186, 188, 196–97, 211; —managers should learn, 73*ff*; follow-up assessment, 205–6; inter-personal and intra-personal, 114, 166, 169, 195; leadership/managerial, 42–43, 164; marketable, 21, 22; non-verbal, 137; practical, 65, 72, 74; psychological, 38; social, 51, 61, 107, 131, 170, 188; soft, 21, 27, 168, 208; supervisory, 205–7, 209; technical, 22, 69, 190; encouraging use on the job, 205–7
sleep disorders, 85, 87
smartness, 21
smoking, 85
social behaviour, 178
social change, 73
social desirability scale, 189, 181
social habits, 104
social intelligence, 101, 104, 106
social interaction, 178
social networks, 187
social relationships, 176
social systems, 88
socio-economic conditions, 154–55
sorrow, 92
spirit, 146
strengths and weaknesses, 34, 74, 78–79, 111, 117, 156; assessment, 196, 204; gender specific, 49
stress, 25, 38, 46, 58, 62, 70, 72, 85–88, 90, 109, 112, 134, 144, 161, 171, 189; management, 51, 88, 91, 153, 158, 168, 175, 181, 192, 200, 202, 209; sources, 87; tolerance, 108; at workplace, 85, 87, 138, 157, 169
success, 20, 25, 26, 42, 47, 57, 60, 69–71, 77, 111, 118, 155, 166, 169–70, 174, 178, 187, 190, 192; at workplace/in job performance, 19, 26–27, 40, 41–48, 51–52, 73, 81, 114–17, 131–32, 168–70, 199; *see also* performance

support, 22, 88, 101, 102, 202, 204–8
surprise, 54
sweating, 77
sympathy, 19, 177

team building, 152
teamwork, 22, 23, 35, 63, 65, 120–21, 178, 209
technical expertise, 26
technology management, 101
tension, 85, 90, 141
thinking process, thoughts, 30, 37, 54, 55, 65, 71, 73, 96, 103, 105, 203; and action, 106
thrill, 31
time management, 191, 200
tolerance, 66, 108, 170
trainer and learner, relationship, 199
training and development, 63, 69–70, 101, 177, 192*ff*
traits, 104, 129–30, 185; emotional, 20, 21; negative, 33; positive, 78; *see also* personality traits
transfer and maintenance, 205–7
trauma, 72, 87
trust, mutual trust, 31, 32, 35, 62, 64, 67, 74, 85, 92, 100, 101, 112, 116, 117, 131–32, 152, 187, 190, 192, 197
turnaround, 92
turnover, 101, 132

understanding, 35–36, 41–42, 77, 91, 106, 114, 116, 121

unhappiness, 55, 141
United States of America, management practices, 122–23, 156, 158–59, 161–65

values and beliefs, 44, 56, 104, 196, 198, 204
vexation, 31
vices, 32
violence, 31, 64, 99
vision, 45, 119–20

wariness, 31
well being, 43, 165–68; multidimensional model, 166
women emotional intelligence, 49, 61; leadership behaviour, 150–51, 158
wonder, 31
work culture, 146
workaholic, workaholism, 72, 97
working relations, 48, 145
workplace, 20, 23, 26, 41, 42, 64, 65, 71, 75, 95, 116, 138; anger at, 97, 100, 131–32, 149, 161, 169, 205–6, 212; applicability of emotional intelligence, 37–38, 176–86, 193, 195; art of influencing people, 95–96; stress, 85, 87, 138, 157, 169, 191; *see also* performance, organisations, success
wrath, 31

About the Author

Dr Dalip Singh is a senior bureaucrat who joined the Indian Administrative Service (IAS) in 1982. He belongs to the Haryana Cadre and has held many important positions in the state and Central Governments.

He obtained his post-graduation in psychology from the University of Delhi in 1978 after which he completed his M.Phil and Ph.D. in psychology with research work in areas such as managerial effectiveness, transactional analysis, leadership and personality. Dr Singh taught at the Faculty of Management Studies, University of Delhi (1980–82) before joining the IAS.

He has the rare distinction of being awarded D. Litt. in psychology for his work on EQ, by Bundelkhand University, Jhansi, India, in 2005.

He is a trained psychologist and an expert on emotional intelligence. He lives in Chandigarh, India, and may be contacted at www.eqindia.com